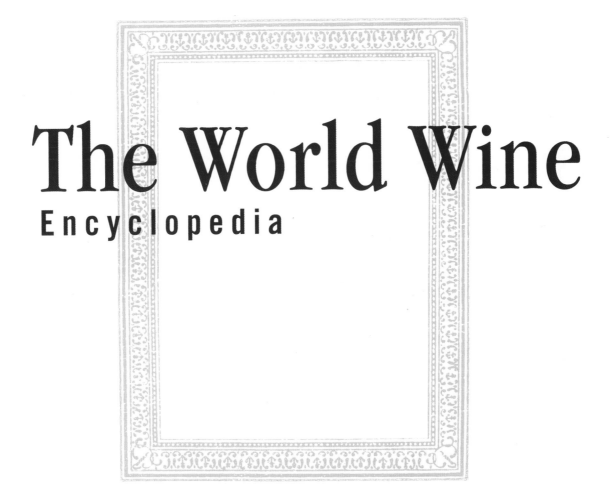

The World Wine
Encyclopedia

This is a Parragon Publishing Book
Conceived and produced by Glitterati Incorporated/www.GlitteratiIncorporated.com

First published in 2006 by
Parragon Publishing
Queen Street House
4 Queen Street
Bath BA1 1HE, UK

Interior Design and Layout by Sarah Morgan Karp

ISBN 978-1-4054-7768-0

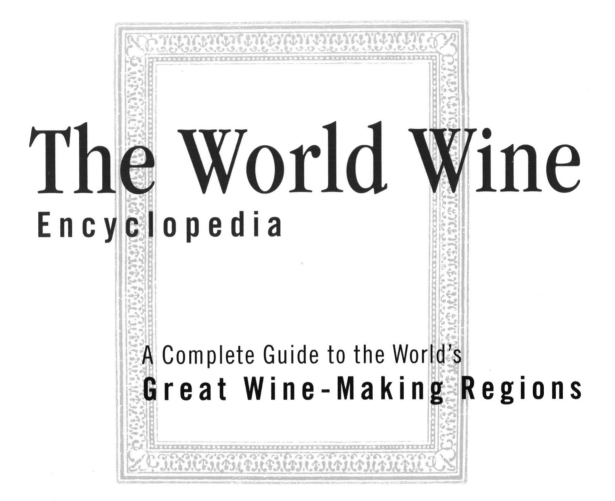

The World Wine

Encyclopedia

A Complete Guide to the World's
Great Wine-Making Regions

by Christy Grosz

p

Dedication
For my parents, who nurtured my love
of wine and food

Acknowledgments
Matt Mack, for being supportive and for
providing the celebratory bottle of Burgundy

Minju Pak, for the opportunity of a lifetime

Table of Contents

Chapter 1

The Basics

For the novice wine drinker, there's no better time than now to begin learning and experimenting with the vintages of the world. Not only are viticultural techniques becoming increasingly more refined, but price barriers for decent wine are all but a thing of the past. While exclusive, renowned vintages remain the purview of the rich and well-heeled, everyday drinking wine is of a much higher quality that it's ever been before — good news for the rest of us.

What follows is a guide that provides need-to-know information about buying and enjoying wine.

Achieving Grapeness When connoisseurs use terms like "intelligent" and "unctuous" to describe a wine, it makes wine, in general, sound incredibly elitist. But the process of creating this ever-so-elegant libation is nothing of the sort. At its heart, making good wine is a combination of agriculture, science and a little bit of arty flair. It requires growing the right grapes under the right conditions, knowing the precise moment to pick, then knowing just how to press, ferment and age the wine in a way that highlights the very best that a given grape can offer. In some more temperamental growing regions, marginal and great can be simply a matter of planting on the right sunny slope instead of a shady valley.

Although there are thousands of grape varieties in the world, they all fall into a basic species called vitis vinifera. Virtually all of the major grapes used for winemaking fall into this category, and vinifera vines are native to Europe and Asia. North American native vines, which include the type that grows the concord grape used for juice and jelly, are called vitis labrusca. While a handful of producers make wine with labrusca, it's not a common practice and generally earns thumbs-down from the wine intelligentsia. The other vine species native to North America is vitis riparia, which is resistant to phylloxera and whose rootstock is used for creating resistant clones of wine-grape vines. Resistant rootstock has been instrumental in helping rebuild wine regions around the world who experience phylloxera outbreaks.

Within the vitis vinifera species are the grapes familiar in almost every country around the world. On the white side are chardonnay, chenin blanc, gewurztraminer, marsanne, pinot blanc, pinot gris, reisling, rousanne, sauvignon blanc, semillon and viognier. When it comes to red, the dominant grapes are cabernet franc, cabernet sauvignon, grenache, merlot, pinot noir, sangiovese, syrah and zinfandel. While any grape will have a distinct, dominant characteristic, a reisling grown in New Zealand will taste radically different from a reisling grown in Germany. Really, comparing flavors of the same grape grown in two different climates is where the fun in wine tasting begins — and where a novice can begin to understand the nuances a glass might contain.

Water Into Wine All wines are made through the same basic process of fermentation. The juice of the grapes is extracted usually by crushing the fruit, separating the stems and seeds (called pips) almost immediately for white wine, but leaving them in contact with the juice for the red wine fermentation process. Whether a grape is red or white, the juice is initially almost colorless, so red wine must remain in contact with the skins for some amount of time to gain its color — this process is called maceration. In addition, stems, seeds, and grape skins contain a substance called tannin that is crucial to providing structure particularly to red wine. However, there's a fine line to walk with tannin — too much and a wine tastes bitter, too little and a wine is unlikely to age well. For very tannic grapes such as cabernet sauvignon, producers often de-stem the grapes before maceration to lessen the tannins, then leave the stems on for grapes with less tannin, such as pinot noir. The "must," as this mixture is known, spends several days to several weeks in a stainless steel tank while yeast converts the grapes' sugar into alcohol. Some higher-end wineries ferment in smaller oak barrels, which is thought to give the wine a creamy texture, but this is usually reserved for white wine. Stainless steel gives winemakers an ability to monitor the temperature during fermentation, and thus allows them more control of the process.

Once the yeast has consumed all of the sugar, fermentation stops and the wine and must are separated. From there, an everyday, drinkable wine might go back into a stainless steel tank, ready for bottling, while a more substantial red wine might go into oak barrels for months or years before bottling.

Shop Smart
Whether it's picking up the right bottle for a special evening or starting a modest wine cellar, choosing the right wine shop can make all the difference. Not only can an educated wine merchant steer novices toward a new region or vintage, but they can provide a wealth of knowledge based on years of tasting. And never stand for a store whose staff seems intimidating or dismissive.

It's also helpful to tap a wineseller in an effort to broaden one's palate and exit the comfort zone. For instance, if you naturally gravitate toward California wine, give the salesperson an idea of what kind of California wines appeal to you, then ask for an Italian or French recommendation. Not only could it provide a new favorite, but it's an easy way to broaden your wine knowledge. After all, learning about wine is tasting wine — not just reading about it.

When it comes to considering vintages, keep in mind that groceries generally stock wines that are meant for drinking immediately. A better wine store will likely have current releases from various wineries, as well as a special storage room for older, hard-to-find vintages.

For U.S. travelers who visit wineries in California or the Pacific Northwest, check into your state's shipping laws before arriving at the winery. Following the Supreme Court's May 2005 direct shipping ruling, which called out-of-state shipping bans unconstitutional, many states lifted some but not all of their shipping regulations. Thirteen states have reciprocal status, meaning that a consumer can ship wine back to themselves or purchase wine from an out-of-state winery. Many states have restricted status, which means that it's not always illegal to ship wine into the state, but there are restrictions. There are still 18 states where it is against state law to ship wine into the state. Six states remain in the felony category — Florida, Georgia, Indiana, Kentucky, North Carolina and Tennessee — which means that any winery that ships to these states would be charged criminally.

Proper Storage

The two biggest enemies of wine are heat and sunlight, particularly for wines that are meant to age in the bottle. Though most wines made today are meant to be drunk within a few years, there are still those bottles that will only improve with age. An improperly stored bottle might not always go bad, but it won't reach its peak, which defeats the purpose of holding on to a bottle for years.

While those fancy wine cooling systems are appealing, they're not absolutely necessary, as long as you keep a few things in mind. First, don't store wine in the kitchen or near any window. It's way too hot for even cheap wine, and the wine will most likely go bad before it's ever opened. Second, not only is heat bad for wine, but drastic fluctuations in temperature can cause the cork to seep. Keeping wine in a low-light room or closet, covered with an old towel isn't pretty, but it works. Third, always keep wine bottles resting on their side. This keeps the cork moist, which is good for the wine and good for the person opening the wine. Fourth, as much as possible keep the wine away from vibration, though its effects are somewhat dubious. And, finally, if you are spending a lot on any given bottle, investing in a cooling system is the best way to protect your wine.

So tending diligently to a bottle for a few years begs the question, when exactly is this thing ready to drink? That's a subject that even the most knowledgeable enthusiasts could spend hours debating over 10-year-old cabernet, but the bottom line is that there's no easy answer. Most wineries can provide a range of years in which a wine is projected to drink well, offering a solid guideline. Often people choose to buy more than one bottle of a given vintage, then try a bottle every year or so to see how the wine changes.

Closure Controversy

With screw-cap finish wines earning less of a stigma these days, the cork-vs.-cap debate might be left to elitist dinner conversation. However, it seems that the much-maligned screw cap still inspires snickers and giggles in mixed company, which only serves to identify the ill-informed in the room. While it's true that the screw cap has closed many an icky wine, these days several producers are using it for some pretty tasty bottles, most notably California's Bonny Doon Vineyard and Three Thieves. Don't fear the screw cap — it closes the wine just as expertly as a cork, and you never have to worry about having a corkscrew on hand. While there is something satisfying about uncorking a bottle, that doesn't mean a screw cap is inferior — it's just different.

Tasting Techniques

Truly tasting wine isn't simply about taking a sip. Factors ranging from the wine's temperature to the glass in which it's served can all affect the flavors one might experience.

As a rule of thumb, white and rosé wine should be chilled, red should be served at room temperature. And while having a full set of chardonnay, bordeaux and burgundy wine glasses seems somewhat excessive for anyone but the most elaborate entertainer, it is important to have one set of all-purpose glasses. The glasses should have a large, wide bowl that narrows near the top to concentrate the wine's aromas. In addition, the rim should be thin, and the glass should have a stem. Glasses don't have to be expensive to be effective, and be sure to buy extra in case a tasting party gets out of hand. The one exception to the everyday wine glass is Champagne, which does require a flute to preserve its bubbly nature in the glass for as long as possible.

Wine novices tend to look askance when anyone discusses the notion of a wine breathing, but it can be crucial in enjoying some wines. As oxygen reaches the wine, it can change the flavor of even the youngest, tartest wine. (However, very old vintages, 20 years or more, generally don't need to breathe. They taste best immediately after opening, and the flavors fade quickly.) The best way to get oxygen to the wine is by decanting, which means pouring the wine into a wide-bottomed carafe. For wines that still contain sediment, a small funnel with a filter can eliminate the solids in the wine.

Once the wine has been opened, the ritual begins. The human tongue can only detect four different types of flavors: sour, sweet, bitter and salty. Wine is, of course, made up of much more than a quartet of notes, so a taster must use the senses of smell and sight to fully appreciate a bottle.

Whether it's a simple glass of wine after work or a fancy tasting party, the best place to start is by pouring a glass, only filling it until the wide bottom is covered. 1) Take note of the color: a darker white wine has usually spent more time in oak barrels; red wine can range from cherry red to almost black, and as it ages in the bottle, it gains a tawnier tone. 2) Give the glass a swirl. This is important for the next part. 3) Nose inside glass, take a big whiff of the wine. Smelling the wine will provide a lot of information about how it might taste. 4) Take a small sip of the wine, allowing it to fill the mouth, paying attention to how it tastes as it makes its way through. Not all wine tastes good right away, so follow this sip with another.

While there is value in having the right vocabulary to discuss wine, the most important element for novices is deciphering the types of wines they enjoy. Taking note of the wine's body or how it feels in the mouth, the dominant flavors and the finish, or the flavors that last a bit longer in the mouth. As you taste more wine, you'll find that certain vintages and flavors are more appealing, which will allow you to find wines across the world that are similarly likable.

White With Fish? Pairing food and wine remains something of an art, enabling each element to complement or contrast certain flavors. And when it's done well, it can make for a transcendent meal. Even when it's not perfect, wine with a meal is still downright pleasant.

The old adage of red wine with red meat and white wine with fish still holds true to a degree, but it is by no means the only way to go. What's more important is keeping in mind that light wines should go with light foods and fuller-bodied wines pair well with heavier food — regardless of a wine's color. If pairing wine with every course seems excessive, choose a wine that complements the main course. Any wine that has good acidity, such as a German reisling or an Italian Chianti, will make food taste better.

When visiting a restaurant, don't hesitate to ask the sommelier for a recommendation that will work for everyone at the table. If there's a particular wine you have in mind that's not on the wine list, ask for a similar bottle. And never worry about giving the sommelier a price range.

Chapter 2
California

The year round warm Pacific Ocean breezes and dry sunny days that make California a perfect vacation destination also make it ideal for grape growing, which is why this West Coast playground produces more than 90% of the wine in the United States. And since the state's moribund wine industry turned around in the late 1960s, California has been producing oaky chardonnay and powerful cabernet sauvignon, not to mention syrah and pinot noir, that are influencing tastes and styles for the rest of the wine world. New and Old World regions are looking to California's technology-savvy, bold winemakers for inspiration and education, while connoisseurs across the country keep an eye out for the next big so-called "cult wine."

The History

For a wine region classified as New World, California has a surprisingly rich history of winemaking. Beginning with the Spanish explorers in the 1700s who began claiming territory from Mexico through what would become California, wine — albeit sacramental — was a part of the west. For more than 50 years, the only wine made was for the missions that were cropping up all over the territory, but by the 1830s, many commercial wineries had opened up for business. And with the California gold rush fueling growth, the wine industry was thriving a couple of decades later. This is when today's foremost regions in the state, Napa and Sonoma, were established as superior grape-growing environments, and many wineries that still exist today — Charles Krug, Buena Vista and Inglenook (now owned by Coppola) — staked their claim in Northern California. With a phylloxera epidemic devastating Europe, the nascent Golden State wine industry saw only shining potential ahead.

Even when phylloxera finally made its way to the Pacific near the end of the 19th century, the resilient state recovered in a matter of a decade. But what crippled winemakers for half of the 20th century was the same thing that stilted thriving wine industries in other parts of the United States at the time: Prohibition. Those 14 dry years reduced the 800 wineries operating in California in the early 1900s to a mere 140 by the end of Prohibition in 1933. It wasn't until the late 1960s that the industry started gaining momentum again —and within a decade it had become competitive with the Old World.

For centuries, the vintages of France have been the examples that winemakers around the world hoped to emulate. So in the 1970s when California's wine industry was pushing to elevate the quality of what it was producing, it was striving to make wine that was exceptional enough to compare to a Bordeaux or Burgundy. No doubt a few discerning Frenchmen had a good laugh when they ran across two Napa Valley wines entered into the Paris tasting of 1976. After all, the California wine industry had been making little more than syrupy, sticky ports just 10 years earlier. But California's Chateau Montelena chardonnay and Stag's Leap Wine Cellars cabernet sauvignon not only entered the competition, they took first place for white and red, respectively. The victory is now commonly referred to as the "legendary Paris tasting of 1976," marking the moment that California leapt onto the world stage of wine.

With the establishment of California's wine industry came a need to regulate labelling, which began in the 1980s with the introduction of American Viticultural Areas (A.V.A.). (Incidentally, the first A.V.A. approved in the States was not in California — it was Augusta, Missouri, in 1980.) Unlike in Europe, the A.V.A. doesn't regulate vine yields or dictate aging, which give the United States more freedom in winemaking, but critics say this diminishes the ability to have a distinctive terroir. According to the Bureau of Alcohol, Tobacco and Firearms, in order for an area to receive official A.V.A. designation, the state must provide the boundaries of the area and geological evidence (soil type, elevation, climate, etc.) that distinguishes the viticultural area from surrounding areas. Of the 185 approved A.V.A.s in the U.S., more than 100 are in California. Some areas include an overarching A.V.A. that has sub-regions within it. For example, the North Coast A.V.A., which doesn't usually appear on any wine label, includes five counties, including all of Napa and Sonoma.

When wineries label their bottles, they are required to follow a handful of government regulations. If a wine has an A.V.A. listed on the label, 85% of the grapes in the wine must originate from the listed A.V.A. If a winery uses the county name instead of an A.V.A. on the label, for instance Sonoma County, 75% of the grapes must come from that county. If the grapes come from all over the state, the label might just say "California." When a vintage is listed, 95% of the wine must be from that year; and when a grape is listed, 75% percent of the wine must be made from that grape. And finally, the government warning about the dangers of alcohol and sulfites has to appear on every bottle made in the U.S.

The World Wine Encyclopedia

The Regions

Consistent weather patterns and a generally friendly grape-growing climate has made California host to most styles and quality levels of wine. Not only do rare premium wines such as Colgin and Harlan originate from this land, but word-of-mouth marketing phenomenon Charles Shaw, or Two-Buck Chuck, is fermented in the Golden State.

Northern California
Although less than 5% of California's wine comes from Napa Valley, this verdant town continues to serve as the touchstone for United States wine production. Napa County, which is the overarching A.V.A., has an extremely varied topography, which is why there are 14 smaller A.V.A.s within the area, including Napa Valley, as well as Diamond Mountain, Stag's Leap District, Oakville, Carneros and Spring Mountain. But what these areas have in common are warm, sunny days and cool evenings.

Chardonnay and merlot are big in Napa, but its bold cabernet sauvignon has been winning awards for decades, and many vintners have established their reputation on blending cabernet with small amounts of cabernet franc and merlot, as well as other French varietals. Some even take the concept further by creating proprietary, meritage-style blends that have less than 75% cabernet sauvignon and generally go by elegant proprietary names such as Niebaum-Coppola's Rubicon, Joseph Phelps' Insignia and Merryvale's Profile, all of which release at around $100 a bottle, with older vintages going for even more.

Single-vineyard designations are also common among Napa vintners, which is why growers such as the Beckstoffer Vineyards and Backus Vineyards pop up on the labels of many wineries in the valley. Because of the growers' ability to deliver consistently excellent fruit, single-vineyard designation is usually a sign of a higher-quality wine with a bigger price tag.

Sparkling wine made in the French style, methode champenoise, has become another facet of Napa's wine production. A far cry from the overly sweet, mass-market bubbly, sparkling wine from such producers as Domaine Chandon, Domaine Carneros, and Mumm Napa Valley (all of which are partly owned by French companies) rival traditional champagne.

While Napa produces some of the best wines in the world, it's not necessarily the best stop for wine novices. Not only are the prices extraordinarily high, but those looking to learn more about wine aren't likely to get the education they want from the often harried pourers. However, just west of Napa is Sonoma, whose style and temperament is far from the maddening crowd of Napa. Instead of traffic jams, $20 wine tasting and a somewhat elitist attitude, Sonoma approaches wine in a down-to-earth fashion, and its wineries usually have time to teach the willing. Fourteen separate A.V.A.s make up Sonoma County, including Russian River Valley, Alexander Valley, Dry Creek Valley and Carneros, which it shares with Napa County and has a stellar reputation for pinot noir and chardonnay.

Nearly every type of grape grows somewhere in pastoral Sonoma, but it excels at pinot noir in Russian River Valley and chardonnay in Alexander Valley. (In fact, one small Sonoma winery called Patz & Hall specializes in only these two wines, and some vineyards grow only these two grapes.) Meanwhile, robust, lush, zinfandels come from all over Dry Creek Valley, and high-quality sparkling wine comes from Green Valley.

As with Napa Valley, single-vineyard wines are popular among Sonoma vintners. The Pisoni Vineyard, Rochioli Vineyard and Hyde Vineyard sell grapes to many boutique Sonoma wineries. These single-vineyard designates aren't quite as high-priced as those in Napa, but they're still expensive.

While Napa and Sonoma get most of the attention, there are several other wine areas around San Francisco worth looking into. Both Mendocino and Lake County (which have 14 A.V.A.s between them) are the northernmost wine regions in California and are known for spicy, mouth-watering zinfandel, while the Sierra Foothills A.V.A. focuses mainly on zinfandel, syrah, and barbera, plus some dessert wines.

Central Coast

The Central Coast is the largest grape-growing region in the state, with a wide variety of terrains and climates. From the craggy cliffs of the Santa Cruz Mountains to the ocean-cooled golden hillsides of Pasa Robles, this beautiful countryside produces some of California's most experimental and palatable wines. Grapevines pepper a good portion of the coastline and valleys between San Francisco and San Luis Obispo, with A.V.A.s ranging from just a few thousand acres to almost 40,000 acres in Monterey County. More than 30 A.V.A.s make up the region — including Livermore Valley, Chalone, Edna Valley and Santa Maria Valley.

Livermore Valley, which is situated inland and south of San Francisco and is Alameda County's only A.V.A., was a center for California's pre-Prohibition wine industry and has been bottling vintages for more than a century. Both red and white grapes thrive in the valley's warm daytime temperatures and cool evening breezes. Although the area's wineries battled aggressive land developers in the 1970s and 1980s, it looks as though vineyards will always be an important part of the valley, thanks to a 1993 law that encourages wine industry growth. New family-owned labels like Murrieta's Well are joining the established historic wineries such as Wente and Concannon.

The Santa Cruz Mountains A.V.A., one of two in Santa Cruz County just north of Monterey, produces some excellent wine, but its rugged mountainsides make it difficult for anyone but the most skilled, dedicated vintners to call this home. However, widely varying microclimates reward the winemakers with the ability to farm grapes that thrive in both cool and warm climates, including cool-temperature loving chardonnay and pinot noir, as well as warmth-craving cabernet sauvignon and zinfandel. Some of the best (and often most interesting) producers in the area include Bonny Doon, David Bruce and Ridge Vineyards.

Directly east of Santa Cruz is another small region called Santa Clara Valley, one of three A.V.A.s in Santa Clara County. Before land developers had their way, the valley had a rich wine history, but these days its reputation is based on being home to Silicon Valley rather than vineyards. J. Lohr and Mirassou, which make some easy-drinking inexpensive bottles, are the two largest producers in the region. David Bruce also purchases grapes from the region for his pinot noir.

Although Franciscan friars planted grapes in the Monterey area more than 200 years ago, it wasn't until the 1960s that it was recognized for its potential as a wine-making region. In addition to boasting some of the state's most breathtaking coastlines, Monterey County has eight A.V.A.s (Arroyo Seco, Carmel Valley, Chalone, Hames Valley, Monterey, San Bernabe, San Lucas and Santa Lucia Highlands) that produce mostly chardonnay, as well as cabernet sauvignon, merlot, pinot noir and syrah. The weather in the county can range from very hot to extremely windy and cold, so wineries tend to make the weather work for them, planting reisling in cooler areas and heartier reds in the warm spots. (Though it's somewhat confusing, it's important to note that Monterey is an A.V.A. within Monterey County, and Monterey County is not an A.V.A.) Of the county's A.V.A.s, Chalone and Monterey are the most noteworthy. Chalone has only one winery that goes by the name of its appellation, while Monterey is home to the wonderful chardonnay and pinot noir of Morgan Winery.

Neighboring San Benito County has five A.V.A.s, but the area seems to sell its grapes to vintners outside of the appellation more than produce wine — with one notable exception. Calera is the only winery in the Mt. Harlan A.V.A., an area so remote that to this day it doesn't have telephone or city electrical service. The winery was founded in the mid-1970s, and has built a reputation for handcrafting vintages of chardonnay, viognier and pinot noir.

Farther south in San Luis Obispo County, wine has been a part of this area's history for centuries, but it remains in the shadow of Napa Valley and Sonoma. Arroyo Grande, Edna Valley, Paso Robles and York Mountain are the four A.V.A.s that make up this mostly cool grape-growing region, which seeing new wineries open at a quick pace. Of the four, Paso Robles, which is the farthest inland, tends to be much warmer and doesn't get the ocean breezes that the other three enjoy. Rich cabernet sauvignon, zinfandel and merlot dominate, but many wineries like to experiment with varietals and blends, such as the Chateauneuf du Pape-style wines from Tablas Creek. And there's a host of affordable, everyday wines from such Paso Robles producers as Castoro Cellars, Peachy Canyon and Tobin James. York Mountain has just one winery, which has been in operation for more than 100 years, while Edna Valley and Arroyo Grande have a handful of establishments known for making excellent chardonnay and pinot noir, such as those of Laetitia, Edna Valley Vineyards and Talley Vineyards.

About 150 miles north of Los Angeles, the winding hills of Santa Barbara County include three A.V.A.s: Santa Maria Valley, Santa Rita Hills and Santa Ynez Valley (one additional designation has been proposed for Santa Maria Bench, which is where Cambria Winery makes its chardonnay, pinot noir and syrah). The scenic Santa Maria Valley is friendly to a wide variety of grapes, which is why producers like Foxen are able to make everything from Bordeaux- and Rhone-style blends to chenin blanc and chardonnay. The Santa Rita Hills, which is the area's newest appellation, makes extraordinary pinot noir and syrah, thanks to morning and evening fog that keeps the area cool. Melville Vineyards and its next-door neighbor Babcock are known for crafting small-lot vintages that reflect the character of the region. The Santa Ynez Valley, which is slightly more sheltered from the ocean's influence, has seen an uptick in traffic recently based on Fox Searchlight's 2004 film "Sideways." Despite this likely fickle trend, the area has a host of excellent wineries that excell with both red and white grapes, many of which are concentrated in the charming town of Los Olivos. Syrahs from Daniel Gehrs and Andrew Murray are worth a taste, while tasty chardonnay and viognier can be found all over the valley, including inexpensive bottles from Fess Parker and Firestone. Rideau also makes a wonderful (and pricey) cuvee called Chateau Duplantier that's worth the extra money.

Southern California
The southern part of the state is known more for restaurant wine lists than indigenous labels, but there are five recognized A.V.A.s spread across four counties. Unfortunately, most of this area has seen its share of pestilence in the form of Pierce's disease in the late-1990s, which killed off nearly half of the vineyards in the largest appellation, Temecula Valley. In addition, some vintners, fearful the disease will return, are selling acreage to developers. But Temecula's more than 20 wineries represent a growing industry in this part of the state, and they continue to elevate the quality of their wine, as evidenced by Stuart Cellars' lovely tropical-tasting Viognier and proprietary cabernet sauvignon blend Tatria. The other A.V.A.s in the region include San Pasqual Valley, which, along with Temecula, is a sub-region in the overarching South Coast A.V.A.; Cucamonga Valley; and Malibu-Newton Canyon, which has a vineyard but no wineries. There's also a non-A.V.A. winery in Los Angeles' exclusive Bel-Air, Moraga Vineyards, whose proprietor grows red and white grapes on eight acres of his hilltop estate. The Moraga Red cabernet sauvignon blend, which comes from the only winery in Los Angeles since before prohibition, sells for about $125 a bottle.

In the Glass

As one of the pioneers of Napa's wine industry in th 1970s, Joseph Phelps Vineyards is credited with re-introducing syrah into the valley, as well as planting a number of Rhone varietals with much success. But what the winery is best known for is a single word: Insignia. This opulent proprietary Bordeaux-style blend of cabernet sauvignon, merlot, petit verdot and malbec was first released in 1978 and represented the valley's first foray into meritage blends. Up to that point, winemakers were focused on single-varietal wines, but with the introduction of Insignia, blending became all the rage. The release of a new Insignia, which generally runs about $90 a bottle for a current release and hundreds of dollars for earlier vintages, still sends chills down the spines of many a wine collector. And unlike many wineries that have since been sold off or absorbed by larger conglomerates, Joseph Phelps is still family-owned. Other Napa Valley and Carneros labels to look for include Acacia, Beaulieu Vineyard, Beringer Vineyards, Cakebread Cellars, Clos du Val, Duckhorn Wine Company, Grgich Hills, Heitz Cellars, Merryvale, Niebaum-Coppola, Pine Ridge Winery, Robert Mondavi, Shafer, Stag's Leap Wine Cellars and Swanson.

Labels with single-vineyard designates have become increasingly popular among winemakers in California. They can count on growers to carefully tend to and harvest the grapes, which is the first step in making high-quality wine. And long-time growers like J. Rochioli Vineyards in the Russian River Valley have found that they can parlay an impeccable reputation for growing grapes into a higher-profile career in making small quantities of wine. Joe Rochioli's career began when he purchased the 161-acre vineyard in the 1930s. His son, Joe Jr., has since spent almost 40 years tending to the vines and selling his family's grapes to well-known Russian River vintners like Gary Farrell, Bannister and Davis Bynum. Joe Jr.'s son, Tom, carried on the tradition when he began making pinot noir, chardonnay and sauvignon blanc from the family's grapes in the mid-1980s, with much success. The Rochioli family's pinot noir sells for about $30 a bottle and offers earthy, black cherry flavors. Other Sonoma Valley, Alexander Valley and Dry Creek Valley labels to look for include Davis Bynum Winery, Ferrari-Carano, Flowers, Gary Farrell, Geyser Peak Winery, Merry Edwards Wines, Patz & Hall, Quivira, Tandem Winery and Williams Selyem.

Although the tasting room at the Central Coast's Babcock Winery resembles little more than a garage, its humble surroundings belie a reputation as one of the best small producers in the area. This family-owned and -operated winery has been nestled against the Santa Rita Hills since 1984, when Walt and Mona Babcock decided to tap their U.C. Davis-graduate son, Bryan, to help start the family winemaking business. Bryan has been handcrafting syrah, pinot noir and chardonnay ever since — and earning many accolades along the way. One taste of the Black Label Reserve Syrah, and any drinker will know why. This succulent, rich wine is filled with black-fruit flavors, as well as peppery notes — all for less than $25 a bottle. Other Central Coast labels to look for include Tablas Creek, Justin, Sanford Winery, Melville Vineyards, Tensley Wines, Beckmen Winery, Daniel Gehrs Wines, Rideau Wines, Bonny Doon Vineyard, David Bruce Winery, Au Bon Climat, Clautiere, Eberle Winery and Andrew Murray Vineyards.

Chapter 3

The Pacific Northwest

Much like the explosive growth of Canada's wine industry, the last two decades have seen wineries popping up in Washington and Oregon at a phenomenal rate. Neighboring Idaho, despite being hampered by a short growing season, also has a small number of wineries. However, even though these regions are discussed in the same breath in wine discussions, they're radically different in terms of climate and signature wine styles.

The History

The first wine grapes made their way to Washington's Walla Walla Valley in 1876, when Italian immigrants planted cinsault vines. Oregon got an earlier start when vines were planted in 1847, and Idaho has been making wine since the mid 19th century. But, as with the rest of the country, all three states found their nascent wineries closing doors during Prohibition. Production ramped back up following World War II, and by the 1960s and 1970s the modern wine industry was born.

Washington, Oregon and Idaho adhere to the American Viticultural Area, or A.V.A., classification, although Idaho has yet to receive any official A.V.A. designations. In addition, Oregon has strict labeling laws compared with its California cousin: For example, in order for a wine to be labeled pinot noir, it must contain 90 percent pinot grapes — in contrast, California requires 75 percent. The state also forbids any naming conventions that could mislead consumers, such as using Burgundy generically.

The Regions

Washington In the formative years of Washington's wine industry, many grape growers assumed that because the state is so far north, colder-climate vines like reisling and gewurtztraminer would fare much better than cabernet sauvignon or merlot. How wrong they were. Thanks to an almost desert-dry climate throughout much of the state, cold mountain rivers and a latitude that provides almost two more hours of sunshine, red grapes thrive. While the Washington whites are considered good, the rich, concentrated flavor of its cabernets and lush fruit of its merlots are changing the way wine lovers think about bottles from this corner of the map.

These days, Washington is considered the most important wine producing region in the Pacific Northwest, comprising more than 360 wineries in eight A.V.A.s, including Columbia Valley, Yakima Valley, Red Mountain, Walla Walla Valley, Columbia Gorge and Puget Sound. Two new appellations — Horse Heaven Hills and Wahluke Slope — were designated in 2005 and 2006, respectively.

The Columbia Valley A.V.A. covers the majority of the east and yields about 60 percent of the state's overall wine production, while the relatively small Walla Walla Valley as well as Yakima Valley tend to produce the best bottles. Puget Sound, which includes the ever-rainy Seattle, is a difficult climate for wine and isn't really a player in the state's industry.

French varietals form the backbone of Washington wine, but this is a place where grape growers like to experiment. Amid the syrah and merlot vines are obscure varietals such as unappealingly named lemberger, which creates a spicy red, and madeleine angevine, which makes a floral white.

Oregon With erratic weather patterns and sporadic sunshine, it really is a wonder that Oregon has managed to carve out a reputation for outstanding pinot noir. which almost all of Oregon's more than 300 wineries grow. Even with an ideal climate, pinot noir is notoriously difficult to cultivate, yet Oregon remains the only major region in the world, outside of France's Burgundy, to specialize in this temperamental grape. Chardonnay and pinot gris make up the white side of the state's wine equation.

Eleven A.V.A.s delineate Oregon's wine industry, but the most noteworthy of these is the Willamette Valley, which, in good years, seems to have the right combination of warmth and moisture to satisfy pinot noir grapes. The Cascade Mountains border the valley on the east, while the smaller Coast Range helps block harsher weather coming from the Pacific Ocean.

To the south of Willamette are the Umpqua and Rogue Valleys, which both have warmer weather and microclimates that favor cabernet sauvignon and merlot. Columbia Valley and Walla Walla Valley, which also extend into Washington, grow a lot of different varietals and are miniscule relative to the other three appellations. As a testament to the region's incredible growth, five new appellations have been added in the last three years: Columbia Gorge, Dundee Hills, Yamhill-Carlton, Southern Oregon and McMinnville.

Idaho Though this mountainous state has fewer than 20 wineries, it has been making wine since for more than a century, building its history with reisling. It has yet to earn any official A.V.A. designations, but the Snake River Valley is likely to be the first to be recognized. Very hot days and cold nights, as well as a short growing season, make Idaho a challenge for grape growers. But many are finding that with careful tending, chardonnay and merlot do well in the state. And those cold nights and early frosts have led to a small amount of ice wine.

The World Wine Encyclopedia

In the Glass

In the tradition of the pioneers who decided to settle here, winemakers of the Pacific Northwest have something of an adventurous spirit that is, perhaps, reflected in the wine they craft.

In Washington, winemaker Gary Figgins started Leonetti Cellars more than two decades ago, after spending his childhood making homemade wine with his grandfather. What was originally an operation out of his home has turned into what is arguably the most well-known winery in the Pacific Northwest, producing some of the most highly-ranked cabernets and merlots in the country. Other Washington labels to look for include Andrew Will Winery, Columbia Winery, Chateau Ste. Michelle, Hogue Cellars, Matthews Cellars, and Snoqualmie Winery.

Oregon's groundbreaking winery, the Eyrie Vineyards, began when owner and winemaker David Lett ignored the advice of his University of California at Davis professors and planted pinot noir in Oregon. Until that moment, no one would have believed that any vinifera vines would survive, let alone thrive, in Oregon. Breaking the rules gave birth to an industry. Lett is known for producing elegant, earthy pinot noir and graceful pinot gris. Other Oregon labels to look for include Adelsheim Vineyard, Archery Summit, Beaux Freres, Broadley Vineyards, Domaine Drouhin, King Estate and Yamhill Valley Vineyards.

Though Idaho's preeminent winery, Ste. Chapelle, has been in business since 1976, an enterprising winemaker from California has spent the last six years working on improving the quality of its merlot, reisling and cabernet sauvignon. Chuck Devlin, who joined Ste. Chapelle in 2000, has thirty years of oenology expertise that he's harnessing in an effort to put Idaho wine on the international map. Other Idaho labels to look for include Bitner Vineyards, Sawtooth Winery and Snake River Winery.

Chapter 4

New York & Other U.S. Regions

The West Coast and the Pacific Northwest produce more than 90 percent of American wine, but the history of winemaking in the United States actually traces back to New York and Virginia in the 18th century (though Dutch colonists tried and failed to plant vines in Manhattan as early as the mid-1600s). Even to this day, all 50 states have some sort of wine industry, with the very frigid North Dakota being the final state in the union to open a winery in spring of 2002. Though few of these wines compete on a world stage, winemakers are using the best of what they have to make palatable creations — such as fruit brandies and wines, dessert-style wines — and planting new hybrid grapes to discover what grows best in the U.S. varied climates.

The History

From the time that the first colony was founded in the United States, enterprising settlers have been making wine for drinking and religious purposes from the native vitis labrusca vines that grow all over the East Coast. Unfortunately, labrusca grapes make better juice than wine, and imbibers who were used to the flavor of European wine couldn't quite get past how strange American wine tasted. Founding fathers like Thomas Jefferson and George Washington experimented with planting European varietals with little success — variable temperatures, humidity, pests and disease were too prevalent to allow the vines to thrive in the colonies. It wasn't until more scientifically inclined Americans began crossing species and importing French hybrids that making better quality wine became reality. By the time of the Civil War, the East Coast had built a small industry based on imported species and hybrids.

But whatever progress the industry made was stopped in its tracks when the temperance movement took hold, resulting in 13 years of dry days for the United States. After Prohibition ended, Ukrainian immigrant Dr. Konstantin Frank, who had successfully grown vinifera vines in his homeland, convinced Charles Fournier of Gold Seal Vineyards in New York's Finger Lakes region that cold wasn't the reason European vines couldn't survive in America: it was pests and disease, which science could control. Fournier, who had worked previously at France's Veuve Clicquot, hired Frank as a consultant, and the pair began grafting European grapes onto phylloxera-resistant American roots. When an extremely cold winter in 1957 failed to kill the grafted vines, they knew they were on the right track. However, it wasn't until the passage of the 1976 Farm Winery Act, which reduced fees and allowed direct sales to consumers, that operating a small winery could be economically viable. By the 1980s, the growth of the wine industry had begun.

A leftover from the Prohibition era looks like it's finally beginning to change: complicated direct shipping laws. Though many states would allow direct shipment to in-state customers, wineries couldn't ship to out-of-state customers. This hampered the distribution of wines outside of their home state, which is why many wines produced outside of California, Washington and Oregon are so difficult to find. However, the Supreme Court ruled in 2005 that if in-state shipping is allowed, out-of-state shipping should also be legal, which could mean that seeing Idaho on the labels in the local wine shop isn't so far-fetched. But change is slow in coming, so be sure to check your state's laws before placing any orders.

The World Wine Encyclopedia

The Regions

New York Though mention of New York calls to mind high rises and yellow cabs, the lush, green state outside of Manhattan is filled with farmland and open spaces. More than 200 wineries spread across four A.V.,A. regions make up New York's wine country: The Hudson River Valley, The Finger Lakes, Lake Erie and Long Island. The state boasts an astoundingly diverse viticulture, growing nearly 50 different varieties of grape. (Incidentally, teetotalers should know that New York is also the largest producer of concord grape juice.)

Carved by the glaciers that created the Great Lakes, the Finger Lakes is the oldest and largest wine region in the state and continues to be the fastest growing. Vines are protected from early frosts and treated to moderate temperatures because of the lakes' insulating effects. Not surprisingly, the majority of wines in the region are cold-weather-tolerant whites, such as reisling, gewurtztraminer and chardonnay. Award-winning ice wine and late-harvest wines also hail from the Finger Lakes.

Reds dominate in Long Island, New York's newest, and perhaps most fashionable, region. Cabernet sauvignon, merlot and cabernet franc benefit from this region's longer growing season and sunny climate, though it's not quite sunny enough to produce full-bodied, lush reds. Though a few wineries exist in the Hamptons on the South Fork, most of the wineries are concentrated in the North Fork part of the island, which is less populated and more protected from the elements.

Virginia With more than 100 wineries in operation, Virginia has come a long way since wine lover Thomas Jefferson's unsuccessful attempts at growing grapes on the land of Monticello. But Jefferson was certainly heading in the right direction because Monticello is one of six A.V.A. regions that make up the state's wine country, including Rocky Knob, North Fork of Roanoke, Shenandoah Valley, Northern Neck George Washington Birthplace, and Virginia's Eastern Shore. White varietals such as chardonnay and reisling dominate, but many of the small, family-owned wineries in the state are experimenting with other white grapes, such as seyval blanc and gewurtztraminer.

Texas This state's wine history dates back to the mid-17th century, when Franciscan priests planted mission grapes, which are closely related to Argentina's criolla. Now the Lone Star state has more than 100 wineries that are producing good chardonnay on the white side, and many critics say that its cabernet sauvignon is the red with the most promise. There are seven A.V.A. regions in the state: Bell Mountain, Escondido Valley, Fredericksburg, Mesilla Valley, Texas Davis Mountains, Texas High Plains, and Texas Hill Country. Wide open spaces with varied terrain and climates give Texas a lot of potential in the wine world.

The World Wine Encyclopedia

In the Glass

Shipping laws make many American wines difficult to track down outside of their home state, but some of them are well worth a little special effort.

Though he's since passed away, the man who helped build New York's Finger Lakes wine country Dr. Konstantin Frank lives on with his eponymous label reisling, as well as the obscure white rkatsiteli, a Russian grape that Frank brought to the States in the 1950s. Other New York labels to look for include Hermann J. Wiemer, Lenz and Standing Stone.

In the heart of Virginia's Monticello A.V.A. region lies Barboursville Vineyards, which became the first vineyard to grow vinifera in the area since Thomas Jefferson's time. Since then it has been quietly building a reputation for successfully making wines from Italian varietals nebbiolo and sangiovese, as well as offering a meritage-style blend called Octagon, which is named after the shape of a room Jefferson designed in Gov. James Barbour's mansion. Other Virginia labels to look for include Horton Vineyards, Linden Vineyards and Prince Michel de Virginia.

Like so many other wine enthusiasts, a trip to France inspired Susan and Ed Auler to establish Fall Creek Vineyards in the Texas Hill Country in 1975. After several years of earning accolades for its sauvignon blanc and chenin blanc, the winemakers decided to create the state's first super-premium cabernet sauvignon, Meritus, which has a touch of merlot and malbec in its composition. Other Texas labels to look for include Cap Rock and Llano Estacado.

Chapter 5
Canada

Although talk of Canada doesn't immediately bring to mind the temperate climates associated with grape growing, this wintry country has been making wine for more than a century, most recently emerging in the last decade as a world-class producer of ice wine, a highly concentrated dessert style originating in Germany. And since Canada's own 1989 Inniskillen Vidal ice wine took home the grand prize at Bordeaux's 1991 Vinexpo, a handful of wineries have been experimenting with production outside of ice wine, slowly but surely building an industry.

The History

Compared with the near millennium's worth of vintner tradition in France and Italy, winemaking in Canada has a relatively brief history. The earliest serious grape growing dates back to a German soldier, Johann Schiller, who retired on a plot of land on the outskirts of Toronto in 1811 and experimented — somewhat successfully — with domesticating some of the continent's wild vines to make wine for his personal use. More than three decades later, Schiller's family sold part of the land to a French aristocrat, Count Justin de Courtney, who expanded the vineyard and lobbied the government to support local wine production. De Courtney's goal was to prove that European varietals could thrive in Canada, and he proved his point when his wine was judged in Paris in 1867 to resemble French table wine better than other foreign attempts. However, de Courtney was never able to build a successful winery, eventually losing his government grants and faded into history.

Around the same time de Courtney was showing the French his North American version of Burgundy wine, a small island in Lake Erie became the home to the first successful Canadian winery, Vin Villa, started by three American farmers in 1866. They founded their business on Pelee Island, the southernmost territory in Canada, and a rival winery quickly followed, going by the name Pelee Island Wine and Vineyard. Bottles from both wineries started selling well when grocer Major J.S. Hamilton began marketing the labels in the United States and Canada. Seeing the success on Pelee Island inspired a few other wineries in Niagara and Toronto to set up shop, as well.

However, while the wine industry was finding its footing in the early 1900s, a temperance movement was gaining strength in Canada. The impending Prohibition era could have easily led to the industry's quick demise, but the Ontario Grape Growers Lobby appealed to the government to allow wine made from Ontario-grown grapes to be exempt from the ban on alcohol. This clever strategy not only saved the industry, but actually saw it expand from 10 wineries in Ontario at the beginning of Prohibition to 67 when it ended in 1927.

While these tentative forays into viticulture certainly built the foundation for today's wine industry, Canadian wine throughout most of the 20th century lacked the refined quality of its European competitors. The vines that are native to the area remain unsuitable for crafting much more than alcohol-laden grape juice, and the country lacked the appellation system necessary to regulating quality. So, in 1989, a resourceful group of wineries in Ontario developed the Vintners Quality Alliance — V.Q.A. more briefly — which regulates the regions and defines the terms used to identify wines (British Columbia adopted the standards a year later). Wines carrying the V.Q.A. stamp meet with the standards of taste and winemaking set forth by the panel.

While V.Q.A. has gone a long way in establishing quality, Canada took its commitment to tradition even farther in 2000 when it pioneered an agreement with Austria and Germany to only produce ice wine the way it's been made for hundreds of years — by letting the grapes freeze on the vine. Other winemakers, such as some in California's Napa Valley, freeze the grapes in freezers, which eliminates the dangers of mold and losing the crop to birds but makes for a less complex wine.

The Regions

Two regions dominate Canadian wine production: British Columbia to the west and Ontario to the east. Though they're separated by more than 2,000 miles, these two provinces produce the bulk of Canada's wine using European varietals and French-American hybrids — and represent the future of the country's wine industry.

British Columbia
Though it's one of the globe's most northern wine regions, British Columbia supports four V.Q.A.-recognized areas: Fraser Valley, Vancouver Island, Similkameen Valley and Okanagan Valley. Most of the wine from this side of the continent originates in Okanagan Valley, whose 62-mile-wide lake creates microclimates that are grape-friendly. While Canada is known for crafting more ice wine than any other country, Okanagan Valley is demonstrating that European varietals such as merlot, cabernet sauvignon, pinot noir and reisling can grow well there, too. Consistently sunny days and cold nights give the area's wine greater acidity, which means better structure and aging potential.

Ontario
Producing about three-quarters of Canada's wine, Ontario has three V.Q.A.s: Niagara Peninsula, Lake Erie North Shore and Pelee Island. Though Ontario's regions are much farther south than those of British Columbia, temperatures tend to be colder, which is why the tempering effects of the Great Lakes, Ontario and Erie, are crucial. In fact, the Niagara Peninsula is a greater distance inland and more susceptible to unseasonal frosts, so the wineries use fans to keep the air circulating in the vineyard during the spring to protect the vines. Niagara's warmer areas heat up quickly in the summer, which allows the fruit to ripen faster and gives it more intense fruit-forward flavors; in the cooler parts, the fruit ripens slowly, giving it the acid it needs for elegance.

In the Glass

Being the newest of the New World wine regions, Canada is still finding its footing among more established regions when it comes to reds and whites. But while many of the early quality issues have been resolved in the last decade, much of the wine this country produces is difficult to find outside of its borders because provincial monopolies heavily mark up the prices. Boutique wineries — such as Okanagan Valley's Quail's Gate, which focuses on perfecting pinot noir, Burrowing Owl Vineyards, specializing in merlot, and Gray Monk Cellars, focusing on nuanced German-style wines — rely mainly on tourism to acquaint the world with their wares.

The one exception to the rule is Canada's most famous winery, Inniskillen. Tourism undoubtedly represents a major part of Inniskillen's business, but the winery's world-class ice wine has been in demand all over the globe for almost 20 years. And for connoisseurs willing to pay the ever-increasing price, Inniskillen's Vidal Icewine is stocked at most high-quality wine shops.

Chapter 6

France

The French are passionate in their belief that the land and climate in which grapes grow are what produces the character of a wine, a notion for which they have just one word to describe: terroir. While this word tends to intimidate the uninitiated and make for seemingly snooty cocktail-party conversation, the idea behind it serves as the heart of the global wine industry. It's really a simple idea that has an exotic-sounding ring: Wine reflects the place that it comes from. It's why California's chardonnay tastes different than Australia's chardonnay. However, no matter how successful the rest of the wine world is in establishing its own distinct terroir and earning accolades for its vintages, every region compares itself to France, the indisputable barometer for quality.

The History

Complementing France's intense passion is a variety of terrains and soil types that are ideal for grape growing, so it's no wonder that the country produces more exceptional wine than any other country in the world.

France's wine history began long before the first millennium when the Greeks planted grape vines in what's currently known as Marseilles. When the Roman Empire spread to France, they too continued spreading viticulture through the southern region. After the fall of the empire, the Middle Ages saw winemaking turn into a mostly monastic pursuit, led by Benedictine monks. By the 13th century, Bordeaux was exporting its vintages to England, and the region was using a rudimentary classification system for its wine by the early 1700s. In 1855, France officially recognized a system based on the price of each wine that serves as the basis for the country's current classification system.

Although France had centuries of winemaking experience by the mid-19th century, its expertise couldn't combat the devastating outbreak of phylloxera that hit the country. The root-eating insect arrived from its native America somewhere around 1860 and ultimately spread through Europe and around the world. The only solution for French grape-growers was to graft French vines onto immune American rootstock. The plague ended up lasting for more than 40 years, resulting in many other countries tearing up vineyards and planting vines with American roots.

Despite the troubles of the 19th century, France was and remains the preeminent wine producing country in the world. In an effort to guarantee the origins of its wine and protect the livelihoods of those producing it, the country developed the Institut National des Appellations d'Origine in 1935. The INAO set the standards the determine categories of wine, and they even regulate some indigenous food products such as cheese and olive oil. The resulting Appellation d'Origine Controlee system, or AOC, serves as the basis of classification for many other countries in the world. France's wine laws are notoriously complicated because in addition to the system the country oversees are regional classifications that can be vexing. Regardless, the AOC has three basic designations that appear on a wine label. While none of these guarantee quality, they're a good start. The highest level, Vins d'Appellation d'Origine Controlee, defines the geographic wine-producing areas, dictates the types of grapes that can be grown there, sets vine yield limits and limits per hectare, determines vineyard and winemaking practices, and even indicates minimum and maximum alcohol levels for certain wines. Vins Delimites de Qualite Superieure (VDQS) represents a slight step down in regulation, with less strict rules about vine yields and alcohol content. And finally, Vin de Pays, which translates to "country wine," has even more relaxed standards, which means the quality can vary, but a good wine store can recommend many highly drinkable and inexpensive bottles from this designation.

The World Wine Encyclopedia

The Regions

The majority of the wine that France produces and that the French drink throughout the year is red, although the peppery rosés of the southern region are ubiquitous in glasses imbibed in the summertime. And while three regions — Bordeaux, Burgundy, and Champagne — are responsible for some of the finest wines in the world, France produces wine in several other regions that are far less prestigious but make wonderful introductions to the country's varied wine styles.

Bordeaux

What's usually most confounding for novices is France's tendency to label wines based on their appellation, rather than the grape that's used to make the wine. While considering how important terroir is to the French makes it a little easier to understand this practice, it still doesn't help a thirsty person in a wine store. Keeping in mind that entire books have been devoted solely to the complexities of Bordeaux, here are a few tips about the region.

The vast majority of wines made in Bordeaux — which is on the southwest side of France, about an hour from the Atlantic Ocean — are red blends made of cabernet sauvignon and merlot, sometimes with cabernet franc, malbec and petit verdot added in small amounts. Traditionally, these wines have a superior ability to age, so much so that prior to the 1970s many were too tannic to drink upon release. But these days, some Bordeaux releases need just a few years of bottle aging to be good.

Bordeaux is the overarching appellation, but the region has several smaller appellations contained within its borders, with those smaller regions divided into even tinier subregions. The best way to decipher a Bordeaux label is to, primarily, know the major appellations, which include Medoc and Haut-Medoc, which are subdivided into Pauillac, Margaux, St. Julien, and St. Estephe; Graves, which includes Pessac-Leognan and is the only appellation in Bordeaux where most chateaus produce white wine in addition to red; Sauternes and Barsac, which are known for their dessert-style wines; St. Emilion; and Pomerol. (In general, if a label just says "bordeaux" without listing a more specific appellation, it's a basic table wine. Some of these can be good everyday wines, so look to a high-quality wine store for a recommendation.) As a rule of thumb, the smaller the subregion, the better the wine. For example, if a label says it originates from Pessac-Leognan, it's likely to taste more refined than one that uses the bigger designation of Graves.

When connoisseurs discuss the wines of Bordeaux, they're generally referring to a handful of extremely high-end chateaus, which is the French term for wine estate or vineyard and is used mostly in Bordeaux. There are five chateaus in Bordeaux that are called "first-growth" or premiere crus and are classified as the very best the country has to offer. This classification dates back to 1855, when Chateau Margaux, Chateau Lafite-Rothschild, Chateau Latour and Chateau Haut-Brion were ranked the best at the Paris Exhibition. (Chateau Mouton-Rothschild was added to the list in 1973, which is the only change since the 19th century.) This initial classification listed chateaus from first-growth all the way down to fifth-growth — there have been additional classifications since 1855, but this is the most famous. And, not surprisingly, these are five of the most expensive labels in the world.

These classified estates often have terms like cru classe (classified growth) and premiere grand cru classe (first great classified growth) on the label, but there are plenty of non-classified estates in the region that make great wine. Referred to as crus bourgeois, which includes more than 200 wineries in Bordeaux, this designation generally offers good-quality wines for a fraction of the price of classified labels.

Burgundy While Bordeaux's classifications and subregions make an intimidating challenge for wine novices, Burgundy (Borgogne to the French) has an archaic land-ownership system that's even more convoluted. But even though this cool-climate inland area just south of Paris has a reputation for being second only to Germany as the most difficult wine region to understand, one thing about Burgundy is easy: the grapes. Pinot noir and chardonnay are the major grapes in the area, and unlike Bordeaux, the wines of Burgundy are never blends of multiple grape types. (In addition, gamay grapes are used for the wines of Beaujolais, which is part of Burgundy, but offers radically different wine. The white grape aligoté is blended with chardonnay to make a regional sparking wine called Cremant de Bourgogne.)

The very heart of Burgundy is based on the notion of terroir, which is where its notoriously difficult land-parcel divisions originate. Rather than defining a vineyard as an estate surrounded by grapevines, vineyards in Burgundy are defined by terroir, which Benedictine monks determined hundreds of years ago. Any given owner might have a couple of rows of grapes here and there throughout Burgundy. Each parcel of land is considered distinctive, and any large part of land could have many different terroirs and could be owned by many different people. For top-tier wines, even if an owner has parcels of, say, pinot noir all over Burgundy, the grapes from those parcels would never be combined. Instead, the grapes from each parcel would be fermented and bottled separated, so as to express the distinct viticulture of each area. Needless to say, terroir is considered sacred in this relatively small wine region.

There are five subregions that make up the A.O.C. of Burgundy: Chablis, Cote D'Or, Cote Chalonnaise, Maconnais and Beaujolais. Of these, Cote D'Or is the most renowned for its vintages, and its wine has four different levels of quality. The basic red and white Burgundy (Bourgogne Rouge and Blanc) are made from grapes grown all over the area and represent Burgundy's most simple wine. From there, a wine that has the name of its village on the label is a step up in quality, for example Gevrey-Chambertin, Pommard, and Beaune are villages in Cote d'Or. The two highest designations, premier cru and grand cru, are similar to the classifications in Bordeaux, meaning they represent the highest quality and the highest prices per bottle. There are more than 200 premier cru designations and only 33 of the most prestigious, grand cru. As for the other regions in Burgundy, Chablis is well-known for making only chardonnay, and crisp, unoaked chardonnay that tends to be expensive; Cote Chalonnaise, which has several premiere cru wines, offers less expensive red and white wine than those of Cote d'Or; Maconnais produces mostly Bougogne Blanc and has no grand crus or premier cru wines; and finally, Beaujolais is most famous for its Beaujolais Nouveau, a fruity wine made from gamay that's meant to be drunk young.

Champagne

There's nothing that says sophistication and luxury better than a glass of fine Champagne. And although plenty of regions both within and outside of France make wonderful bubbly wine, only sparklers created in the boundaries of the chalky cliffs of Champagne can legally take on the name.

Strangely enough, the wine that's become essential to every special occasion was created somewhat by mistake. Because Champagne is generally cooler than most wine regions, the wines made in the fall would end up too cold by winter for the yeast to finish its fermentation properly. In the spring, the yeast would warm up and begin its foamy fermentation anew, giving the wine a sparkling quality. In the 17th century, a monk named Dom Perignon began looking for a way to stop the bubbles and improve the flavor. Though he perfected a technique for making white wine from red grapes, he never succeeded in ridding Champagne of its characteristic bubbles. So the winemakers of Champagne began embracing their fizzy fortunes and perfecting their winemaking technique.

There are five major vineyards in Champagne: Cote de Blancs and Cotes de Sezanne, both of which grow chardonnay; Montagne de Reims, which grows pinot noir and pinot meunier; Vallee de la Marne, which grows pinot meunier; and The Aube, which grows pinot noir. Champagne classifies its wine based on the quality of vineyards, grading vineyards on a percentage scale ranging from 100% for its 17 grand cru villages, 90% to 99% for premier cru, down to 80% for the less favored villages. This grading scale doesn't appear on the label, so it's important to note that wines from Montagne de Reims, Vallee de la Marne and Cote de Blancs are considered the most prestigious because these three areas comprise all of the grand cru vineyards.

Most high-quality sparkling wines anywhere in the world are made using Champagne's methode champenoise, which requires two separate fermentations and a whole lot of complex procedures along the way. There are wines from just three grapes that are blended into a bottle of Champagne — chardonnay, pinot noir and pinot meunier — but the blend could have dozens of individual wines made from various lots of grapes. (Much like a Burgundy wine, all of the lots are kept separate during the initial fermentation to preserve the characteristics of terroir.) Once the winemaker decides on a blend, a mixture of yeast and sugar is added to each bottle of wine, and the bottle is corked. As the yeast eats the sugar, it produces more alcohol and carbon dioxide. Because there's no escape route for the carbon dioxide, it dissolves into the wine, eventually resulting in bubbles. The bottles rest for about a year, at which point the yeast has to be removed through a process called riddling. Either by hand or machine, the bottles are turned and rested on an increasingly steep angle until they're upside down with all of the yeast cells in the neck of the bottle. Then the neck of the bottle is frozen, so when the bottle is turned upright and the cork removed, the yeast neatly shoots out the top. The bottle is topped off with additional wine and some sugar (called dosage), then recorked.

A non-vintage Champagne, which is the least expensive type, is a blend of dozens of still wines from various years and spends about 15 months aging in the bottle. A vintage Champagne, one with a year listed on the label, is a blend of the best still wines a producer makes and spends at least three years aging in the bottle— these are only made in excellent harvest years. The highest quality level, the prestige cuvee, blends superior wines and is usually a vintage — these are also only made when the winemaker believes the quality is excellent. The style of Champagne can range from crisp and acidic to creamy and rich, with varying levels of dryness.

There are a few of exceptions to the rule in Champagne: blanc de blancs, blanc de noirs and rosé. With a name that translates to "white from whites," Blanc de Blancs Champagne eschews the chardonnay-pinot noir-pinot meunier formula, using 100% chardonnay. Blanc de Noirs (white from reds) is a slightly pink-hued Champagne made only from red grapes and is rare in the region. Rosé Champagnes are also rare and expensive, but well worth seeking out. They're usually made by adding a small amount of pinot noir to the bottle just before the second fermentation, although a small amount of houses produce it by letting the blended wine make contact with the skins of the pinot noir just long enough to pick up some color.

Sparkling Conversation

A look at the varying levels of dryness found in the bubbly

Though it's called cava in Spain and Greece, prosecco in Italy, and Champagne and cremant in France, sparkling wines across the world make any everyday event seem like a celebration. And while Champagne is still considered the very best sparkler in the world, other regions and countries have palatable effervescent wines that compete well with their French counterpart.

Before making a purchase, however, it's important to be familiar with the varying levels of dryness, which aren't aren't always intuitive for the uninitiated imbiber. Bubbly the world over generally falls into three categories based on the sugar content of the wine: brut, extra dry and sec, or sweet. Brut is the very driest of wines, with anywhere from one-tenth of a percent of sugar up to 1.5%. Extra dry has a somewhat misleading name because these wines are sweeter than brut, with up to 2% sugar. Sec has up to 3.5% sugar, and its counterpart, demi-sec, is significantly more syrupy with up to 5%. Served only as a dessert, the very sweetest sparkling wine is called doux and has more than 5% sugar content.

Once you bring home the right bottle, be sure to chill it before serving and take care in removing the cork, slowly twisting it out of the bottle. Despite everything you see in old movies, the less noise a cork makes on the way out of the bottle, the better. You'll end up keeping more of the precious bubbles in the wine, and that's really what it's all about.

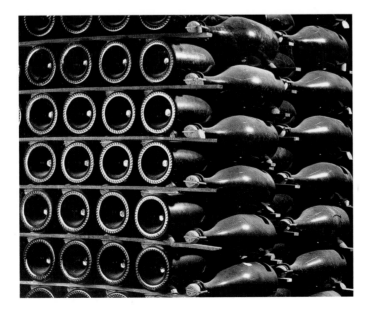

France

The World Wine Encyclopedia

The Rhone

While Bordeaux and Burgundy supply the collector with rare, expensive vintages, the Rhone has a plethora of earthy reds that make loving wine worthwhile for the casual aficionado. Though the Rhone's exotic-tasting, bold wines are not always without a hefty price, there's something about the region that can make even a novice feel like they're discovering something new.

The appellation takes its name from the river that divides it into two distinct — and very different — northern and southern regions. The more prestigious northern regions proves the adage that the more grape vines struggle, the better the resulting wine, as the northern Rhone is characterized by a series of vineyards precariously perched on rocky plateaus and steep slopes above the river. Cold, hard winters and sunshine only in areas with southern exposure mean that grape growers are always keeping their fingers crossed. Heady, spicy red wine, made solely from syrah, dominates the region, with the most coveted originating in Hermitage and Cotes-Rotie, although plenty of other great bottles come from St. Joseph, Cornas and Crozes-Hermitage. Viognier from Condrieu and Chateau-Grillet, a tiny appellation in the region, are also worth checking out, but expect to pay a hefty price. Overall, the prices of northern Rhone wines reflect the fact that you can almost never go wrong taking home a bottle.

The southern Rhone has a decidedly more varied palette of red and white grapes from which to choose, although red still dominates. With a sunbaked, Mediterranean climate and the cooling effects of the wild Le Mistral wind, this region blends the dominant grape grenache with a host of other types, such as mourvedre, cinsault, carignan and syrah to create a wine that has been characterized favorably as dark and untamed.

Of the six major areas within the south, the wine made in the region of Chateauneuf-du-Pape earns the most raves. The odd moniker translates to "new castle of the pope," which hearkens back to the 14th century when the pope lived in Avignon, France, rather than Rome. The pope eventually moved on, but the name stuck to a wine with unexpected flavors like leather and herbs. Though a high-quality Chateauneuf-du-Pape can cost upward of $75, its ability to satisfy makes it worth spending extra for a special occasion.

Exotic spice and bold fruit characterize other regions in the area, as well, including Gigondas, which is generally considered a more robust version of Chateauneuf-du-Pape; Vacqueyras, a peppery syrah-dominated blend; Tavel, which produces lovely fruity rosés; and Beaumes-de-Venise, which specializes in sweet fortified wines made from the muscat grape. Almost three-quarters of Rhone wine carries the Cotes du Rhone or Cotes du Rhone Villages, which makes them the most reasonably priced in the region. However, these two designations can be somewhat hit or miss, so don't pick a bottle simply based on price — look to a knowledgeable wine store for guidance.

France

The Loire Just about the only things uniting the Loire as a wine region are the river after which it is named and the cool climate that influences its grapes. Although the wines produced here range the full spectrum — red and white, dry and sweet, still and sparkling — not all of the Loire's vintages make it to shelves around the world, so the Loire's global reputation is for exceptional white wine made from sauvignon blanc and chenin blanc.

Being nearly as far north as Champagne, the Loire relies on the cooperation of the weather to ensure that its grapes ripen sufficiently in the northern chill. The crisp acidity that characterizes the regions white wine and pairs so well with so many types of meals can easily become thin and watery in the wrong vintage. A knowledgeable wine store can help navigate this terrain, but top producers in Sancerre and Pouilly-Fumé are reliable buys. These wines don't improve with aging, so it's best to find a good bottle and drink it within a few months. The right vintage with the right meal can demonstrate the best that sauvignon blanc has to offer.

More than 50 appellations make up the Loire, but most fall into three diverse sections: Muscadet, the Middle Loire and Eastern Loire. Muscadet is the closest area to the Atlantic Ocean, and it's known for making one wine that goes by the same moniker. Made from the melon de Bourgogne grape, this dry white pairs well with seafood. One term to look for on a Muscadet label is "sur lie," which means that the yeast was left in contact with the wine for several months before bottling, giving it somewhat more structure than it would otherwise have.

The Middle Loire, which includes Anjou-Saumer and Touraine, is home to the dry chenin blanc of Savennieres, which draws praise for its intense mineral qualities, and Quarts de Chaume, a dessert-style wine made from chenin blanc. Most of the wines made in Anjou-Saumer are somewhat sweet rosés, although Rosé de Loire offers a fruity, drier alternative. In Saumer, which is a town between Anjou-Saumer and Touraine, sparkling wine leads production. Generally, the bubbly is labeled as Cremant de Loire or has a specific appellation. Just east of Anjou-Saumer, Touraine is reliable for food-friendly wine, including the white chenin blanc-based Vouvray and the cabernet franc-based Chinon. Bourgueil and St. Nicolas de Bourgueil, two other high-profile appellations within Touraine, provide a variety of good go-to reds made from cabernet franc, as well.

Sauvignon blanc is the dominant grape in the Eastern Loire, and some of France's most famous interpretations call this their home. Sancerre and Pouilly-Fumé, among others, are held up as the standard by which all of the world's sauvignon blanc is measured. Other notable, and less expensive, appellations within this region include Menetou-Salon, Quincy and Reuilly.

Languedoc-Rousillon

Although it's the largest wine-producing region in the country and many of its vines date back centuries, Languedoc-Rousillon has only in the last decade or two gained a reputation for its vintages. These days this sun-drenched Mediterranean Sea-influenced region is a bargain-hunter's paradise, offering a wide selection of good-quality, food-friendly bottles.

Reading the label of Languedoc-Rousillon wines can be tricky. Some wines take on the name of their originating village, such as Minervois or Corbieres, some simply go by the name of the grape and some have a proprietary name. The wines that take on the name of their appellation are, in general, Mediterranean-style blends including mourvedre, syrah and grenache. The wines that have a proprietary name or grape listed on the label are classified as Vins de Pays d'Oc and are usually blends of a single varietal that might have grown in several different vineyards.

Plenty of drinkable wine comes from this region, but there are five major appellations that are the most well-regarded: the villages of Corbieres, Faugeres, Minervois and St. Chinian, as well as the larger region Coteaux de Languedoc. While spicy, herbal reds dominate across this part of the country, Languedoc-Rousillon also makes some white wine from chardonnay and viognier, a sparkling wine called Cremant de Limoux, a sweet fortified wine called Banyuls, and some rosé.

Alsace

At times in its history, Alsace has been a part of Germany and France. And although its geographic and philosophic heart settled in France, its Teutonic neighbor to the east continues to provide a significant influence on Alsace's approach to wine.

Although it's not as far north as Champagne, Alsace offers a cool climate for grape growing, and the overwhelming majority of the vines planted the region are white. Five leading grapes — riesling, gewurtztraminer, muscat, pinot gris and pinot blanc — flourish here, producing dry lively wines that partner well with food. (The only red grape grown here is pinot noir.) About a tenth of the wine produced is the sparkling Cremant D'Alsace, which is made using methode champenoise, though legally it cannot be labeled as such. Alsace wineries also make two late-harvest concentrated wines called Vendange Tartive, which can be sweet or dry, and Selection de Grain Nobles. Both of these require botrytis or "noble rot" to concentrate the sugars, so they're only made in particularly favorable years and are rare.

The region's winemakers focus so strongly on the characteristics of the grape and the land where it's grown — somewhat of a different take on terroir — that they list the grape right on the wine label. For this reason, Alsace's wine labels look more like those of Germany than France. Although most wineries in the region make several wines that fall into a few different levels of quality, there's one designation that denotes the best: grand cru. There are 50 vineyards with this official designation, though not every producer uses the term on the label because it's somewhat controversial. Some choose to use a proprietary name for their best wines or name them after the vineyard instead.

Provence Perhaps it's the lure of the Mediterranean Sea or the scent of lavender in the air, but Provence has never really been a region that focuses much on high-quality vintages. Instead, both the locals and tourists seem to be just as happy quaffing light rosés in the heat of the summer and drinking everyday reds the rest of the year. However, while connoisseurs generally look to more prestigious regions, novices will find that this part of France's coastline is a great source for inexpensive, very drinkable bottles.

Hot, sunny days and the wild northern wind Le Mistral make for bold, spicy reds and peppery rosés, both of which are generally based on grapes such as mourvedre, grenache, cinsault, syrah and cabernet sauvignon. Provence has a handful of notable A.O.C.s, including Bandol, Cassis, Coteaux d'Aix-en-Provence and Cotes de Provence, which is the largest.

In the Glass

Expertly choosing a bottle of French wine requires some knowledge about the styles and reputions of the A.O.C.s, as well as the individual villages. For that reason, the novice is better served by consulting a high-quality wine shop whose employees have skill in individual regions. Pick up a few bottles in a region whose style sounds exciting and start tasting.

One curious tradition within France's wine industry that further complicates the information that ends up on a label is the negociant, or wholesaler. These are brokers who purchase grapes from various parcels of land, then make and market their own wines under their own labels. The practice was much more popular prior to the 1960s, before small growers decided to make and bottle their own wines, which led negociants to begin growing their own grapes. Negociant wine is considered somewhat lackluster because it doesn't express a specific terroir, though some of the larger houses such as Bouchard and Louis Jadot offer consistent quality year to year.

Although tradition is an intrinsic part of France's culture, there's one producer in Burgundy whose business decisions represent a new way of thinking about terroir. Like so many other family-held wineries in France, Domaine Joseph Drouhin has been growing grapes and producing coveted wine in Burgundy for more than 100 years. Domaine Drouhin owns vineyards all over Burgundy, with several Premier Cru and Grand Cru vineyards in Chablis, Cote du Nuit and Cote de Beaune to its credit. But while Drouhin's wine is steeped in Burgundy's winemaking history, the company's influence isn't limited to its home country. Recognizing Oregon's potential in growing Burgundy's sole red grape pinot noir, Domaine Drouhin Oregon opened its doors in 1988 and has been earning critical acclaim ever since. Domaine Drouhin is just one of dozens of French wine companies that have made forays into the New World bringing along Old World customs.

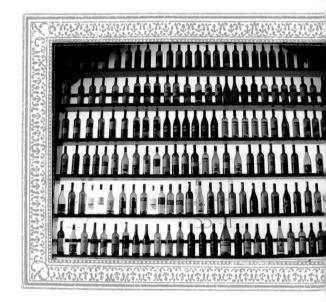

Known for delighting in all things epicurean, Italians never let a meal hit the table without uncorking a bottle of wine to accompany it. While oenophiles from around the world flock to Piedmont and Tuscany to seek out the finest high-end vintages, affordable table wine represents a crucial part of everyday culture — and it can be so tasty that tourists rave about it once they return home. But with more than 20 distinct winemaking regions and close to a million registered vineyards, Italy's wine industry challenges the knowledge of even the most seasoned collector. However, novices, armed with some basic information about the country and its wine culture, can learn to navigate the cellars and vines of this Mediterranean food and wine haven with relative ease.

The History

The Italians' love affair with the grape dates back more than 3,000 years, but the country hasn't always had a reputation for producing world-class wines.

Though Piedmont and Tuscany began building their wine traditions in the 19th century, the 20th century brought war and economic hardship, including a devastating outbreak of phylloxera, which nearly killed the burgeoning wine industry and set the stage for decades of less-than-stellar wine. In order to combat the food shortages following World War II, grape growers began planting high-yield vines, rather than selectively cultivating grapes that would produce high-quality wine. Exporting the plonk — a slang term for low-quality wine — to France helped give Italy a boost in the post-war years, but reversing the downward trend in grape quality would take decades.

Tannic Chianti in the straw-covered bottle — the harsh flavor of which even saucy pizza couldn't mask — represented what most of the world associated with Italian wine until the mid-1970s, when a viticultural shift began elevating the industry. Young Italian winemakers, seeking to improve the quality of their wine, looked at the innovations France and California had made in techniques and were inspired to update outdated wineries. They also revived Italy's abundant indigenous varietals, recognizing that some of these nearly extinct vines could help set the flavor Italian-grown grapes apart from the rest of the wine world.

And, most importantly, the industry's wine regulation began catching up with the rest of the world. Implemented in 1966, the Denominazione di Origine Controllata (D.O.C.) — a classification system that provides basic controls on wine quality — offered a way to distinguish better-quality wines from vino de tavola or table wines, but many found it to be not strict enough. Therefore, Denominazione di Origine Controllata e Garantita (D.O.C.G.) — which denotes the most elite class of Italian wine and was established in 1980 —provides even tighter regulations, demanding longer aging times and lower yields to ensure the highest quality. To date, there are 24 wines that have been awarded D.O.C.G. status, and more than 300 have D.O.C. designations.

Though D.O.C.G. was conceived to indicate the very finest wines Italy has to offer, the winemaking rules that the standard calls for still adhered to more traditional, sometimes centuries-old, methods. Determined to shake up the industry and build on Italy's heritage, a renegade group of winemakers, who found the D.O.C.G. regulations constricting, emerged in the 1980s. And they broke the rules where ever they could: By blending the dominant grapes of the region such as Sangiovese with the grapes of imported Cabernet Sauvignon vines and aging these new wines in French oak barrels instead of traditional casks, these experimentational winemakers ended up creating luxury-style labels whose quality and prices were comparable to coveted French Bordeauxs and Burgundies. Though these so-called super-Tuscans were initially given table wine classification because the wineries didn't follow D.O.C. rules, legislators revised the law in the 1990s to give some super-Tuscans D.O.C. designation and others a new table wine classification, Indicazione Geografica Tipica (I.G.T.). I.G.T., is a step above table wine, but below D.O.C., and the quality at this level can be inconsistent because of the designation's catch-all tendency. Not surprisingly, the government continues to refine the regulations.

The Regions

Incorporating some of the world's most varied terrain and wine-producing techniques, Italy offers a vast array of styles from which connoisseurs can choose. In fact, the country's climates and styles are so complex that most experts refer to Italy as a series of regions, rather than attempting to characterize the country's overall industry. Of course it's difficult to sum up any country's wine industry by highlighting just a few representative areas, Italy has become unquestionably defined in the last few decades by the bottles coming out of Tuscany and Piedmont.

Piedmont and the Northwest

Residing at the foot of the Alps, Piedmont — whose name translates literally to "foot of the mountain" — is the largest winemaking region on Italy's mainland, and almost 20% of all recognized D.O.C. and D.O.C.G. wines come from this area. While three red grape varietals dominate the region, including barbera and dolcetto, the complex fruit flavors and rich tannins of nebbiolo have become the epitome of a Piedmontese wine. Incidentally, nebbiolo gets its name from the fog (nebbia) that covers the hills in Piedmont.

Though the slow-ripening, temperamental nebbiolo vine grows throughout Piedmont, the tiny villages of Barbaresco and Barolo stand out among its producers, creating some of the most coveted wines in the world and representing two of the first with D.O.C.G. status. Unlike winemakers in Tuscany, who enjoy blending and experimenting, the vintners on these densely packed hillsides prefer to craft with the utmost care single-variety vintages with enough structure to enable years, sometimes decades, of aging. They're also a good example of how one type of grape, when grown in two types of soil and turned to wine using varying methods, can yield distinctly different-tasting wine. Barbaresco is considered the more refined and graceful of the two (and there's far less of it produced each year), while Barolo tends to be stronger and more robust. Other well-known wines made from nebbiolo include Gattinara and Ghemme, both of which are in the cooler Alpine region, making for a heavily tannic, harsher wine that requires blending to make them softer.

While the world has fallen in love with Barolo and Barbaresco, Italians tend to quaff Barbera on a regular basis. The hardy vine has been planted throughout Piedmont since the 13th century, but it wasn't until the viticultural revolution in the 1980s that it began receiving the barrel-aging that it deserved. The best versions of Barbera, which have a soft texture and lovely fruit, originate from Alba and Asti.

However, as popular as Barbera is, nothing compares to the easy-to-drink character of Piedmont's third prevalent grape, dolcetto. This light-bodied, low-acid wine is great for everyday imbibing, with some of the best wines coming out of Alba and Dogliani. Dolcetto is best drunk young, for the most part.

Red wine is, without a doubt, what Piedmont is known for, but white wine has its own place in the region, as well. The village of Gavi makes wine from the cortese grape, which is native to the area and makes a prized crisp, mineraly wine; and Roero grows the arneis grape, which produces a dry, fruity wine. But perhaps the most universally recognized white wine style coming out of the country is Asti, a semisweet, low-alcohol, sparkling wine made from the moscato grape that often has "spumante," meaning foaming, appended to its name. It earned a deserved reputation for being an overly sweet version of Champagne when cheap versions began making their way into the United States after World War II, but the high-end versions made today are well worth investigating. A more refined version of asti, called moscato d'Asti, is a traditional drink for Italians on Christmas.

Tre Venezie (The Northeast) A trio of regions commonly referred to as the
Tre Venezie (or Three Venices)—Trentino-Alto Adige, Friuli-Venezia Giulia, and the Veneto—make up the Northeastern region of Italy's wine map. Because Trentino-Alto Adige and Friuli-Venezia Giulia were once a part of neighboring Austria, strong Teutonic influences are a part of this area's culture, resulting in some of the country's best white wines, as well as interesting reds and lively sparklers.

Although Trentino-Alto Adige are joined by a hyphen, these two regions couldn't be more different in terms of population. Alto Adige, which still has a German-speaking majority and identifies more with Austrian culture, reluctantly joined Italy after World War I. Meanwhile, Trentino is decidedly Italian in language and identity. Where the two meet is in their German-influenced approach to winemaking, taking place on the steep hillsides of narrow, glacier-carved valleys.

Vines cover almost every part of Trentino-Alto Adige, which has been making wine since the Roman Empire. Almost 20 different grape varieties are planted here, and many wines are named after the grape, rather than the traditional village naming. Some bottles even carry Italian and German names for the wines, making for a crowded-looking wine label but one that wine novices can decipher easily.

Chardonnay is the most important white grape grown in the region, and its flavor is as varied as a California chard, running from fresh, dry flavors to oaky and heavy. Some wineries also specialize in the floral and intensely flavored traminer, which German wine fans know as gewurztraminer. Other whites come from pinot bianco and pinot grigio.

Though the Trentino-Alto Adige is renowned for its whites, plenty of classic red grapes are made into quaffable wine, despite its colder northern location. From cabernet franc, cabernet sauvignon, and merlot to varietals native to Italy, such as lagrein, marzemino, schiava and teroldego, grapes grown in this region tend to yield spicy, tannic wines. Though schiava and a few other grapes are used for making inexpensive blends, most wines from Trentino-Alto Adige are single-varietal.

Friuli-Venezia Giulia, commonly shortened to Friuli, also has some single-varietal wines, but this is where some of the best white blends originate. Even though almost half of what Friuli produces is red, its reputation as a prestigious wine region is based on white wines made from chardonnay, pinot bianco, tocai, pinot grigio, ribolla gialla (a native vine), and sauvignon blanc. Sunny Alpine foothills and warm breezes from the Adriatic Sea give Friulian white grapes plenty of time to ripen, resulting in fruity, full-bodied wines. In fact, the pinot grigio is far fruitier and richer than what most casual wine drinkers are used to ordering by the glass at a midrange Italian restaurant. More than 30 red and white varietals are planted here, and almost 40 percent of Friuli wines have D.O.C. status.

As one of the largest wine producers in terms of volume, the Veneto is home to some of Italy's most recognizable styles of wines: Soave, Valpolicella and Bardolino. Unfortunately, ubiquity doesn't necessarily guarantee any level of quality, so most of these wines have a reputation for tasting anywhere from so-so to bad. But for Soave and Valpolicella in particular, the quality is most assuredly on the uptick, though many connoisseurs still prefer to steer clear of these simple wines.

Where the Veneto shines is with a unique-tasting sweet wine called Amarone. Although the Veneto tends to be too cold to produce the ripe grapes needed to make rich reds, the Italians employ a method called recioto, which makes possible the thick, syrupy Amarone. Amarone is made from most of the same grapes that go into Valpolicella — corvina, molinara and rondinella — but instead of picking at the peak of ripeness, the grapes used in Amarone are left on the vine for a little longer until they're overripe. Then the grapes spend up to four months drying in bunches, until they've lost most of their water and the sugars are concentrated. The raisin-like fruit is crushed and fermented, with the resulting wine receiving oak-barrel aging for up to five years. Because of the labor involved in making this wine, the price can be high, but fans say the heady, port-like flavors make it worth the extra cash.

Tuscany and the Central Region

Although the country has several central regions of note — such as Emilia-Romagna, Marche, Umbria, Abruzzi and Liguria — the red wines of Tuscany tend to overshadow everything else around them. In addition to being a place where winemakers' experimentation resulted in the coveted Super Tuscan wine style, Tuscany is home to three important styles of wine that have helped build Tuscany's reputation as the epitome of what Italian wine has to offer and were among the first to be recognized with D.O.C.G. status in 1980. This trio of Chianti, Brunello di Montalcino and Vino Nobile di Montepulciano are all made from the sangiovese grape, which, along with cabernet sauvignon, represents most of what the region grows.

Coveted by wine collectors, Brunello di Montalcino takes its name from a clone of the sangiovese grape, called brunello, and is known for its ability to age for a long time. By law, Brunello must age for four years, with at least two in oak; Brunello reserva is required to age for five years, with two and a half in oak. The resulting wine has complex black fruit aromas and flavors, as well as hints of chocolate and leather.

While Chianti had a reputation for being inexpensive and quaffable in the last century, it was hardly renowned for its ageability or complexity. But beginning in the 1970s, a small group of winemakers decided to throw out the traditional Chianti recipe — which was developed in the 1800s by Baron Bettino Ricasoli, who blended red and white grapes to improve drinkability — and began making pure sangiovese, with no white grapes to be found. Though the resulting wines were spectacular, they didn't adhere to the D.O.C. guidelines for Chianti, so they were given proprietary names like Tignanello and Ornellaia instead — and called Super Tuscans by the wine cognoscenti. When the district was elevated to D.O.C.G. status in 1984, the rules that a winemaker must follow in order to label a wine as Chianti were improved, giving some of these pioneering winemakers the opportunity to give their experimental wines the official D.O.C.G. Chianti name. However, many have held on to the cachet that being a renegade Super Tuscan offers and have chosen to stick with their proprietary monikers. Unfortunately, it makes Italian wine all the more complicated for the uninitiated.

Chianti is divided into seven sub-zones — which include Chianti Classico, Chianti Rufina, Colli Fiorentini, Colli Aretini, Colli Senesi, Colline Pisane and Chianti Montalbano — but Chianti Classico is by far the most important and has its own D.O.C.G. designation. When a label says Chianti Classico, the wine, by law, is made from 75% to 100% sangiovese; if a wine isn't totally sangiovese, the other 25% can include up to 15% cabernet sauvignon and/or merlot, up to 10% canaiolo, and up to 6% the white grapes trebbiano or malvasia. The best wines from this region are called Chianti Classico Riserva and are only made in the highest quality vintage years. By law, the Riservas are aged two years in wood (most in French oak) and three months in the bottle, resulting in a heady mix of earthy, spicy flavors.

Like Brunello and Chianti, sangiovese is the primary grape in Tuscany's Vino Nobile di Montepulciano, though Vino Nobile uses its own sangiovese clone called prugnolo. Also like its cousins, Vino Nobile must be aged in wood for two years, and the riservas must be aged in wood for three. Many wine fans look to the younger sub-zone of Rosso di Montepulciano for more reasonably priced interpretations of Vino Nobile di Montepulciano.

In Tuscany, red wine Carmignano and white wine Vernaccia di San Gimignano are also worth noting, but it's the unique Vin Santo that provides the real allure beyond the hearty reds of this area. In much the same way that the grapes of a French Sauternes shrivel on the vine to concentrate flavors, Vin Santo is made by drying white grapes for three to six months until about half of the fruit's liquid has evaporated. The raisin-like grapes are then crushed and fermented slowly in sealed oak barrels situated in a warm room for three to five years. The resulting wine can be dry or very sweet, depending on the producer, and it's typically served after a meal with biscotti. Not surprisingly, this labor intensive stuff is expensive.

The Southern Region
Although vineyards cover the majority of the Southern part of Italy, very few wines of quality come from here, most are table wines meant to be drunk shortly after bottling. However, with all of the modernization taking place everywhere else in the country, a viticultural shift might not be too far off.

Campania, Apulia, Basilicata and Calabria make up the major regions on the southern mainland, while the islands of Sicily and Sardinia have their own unique wine styles. Of the four regions grouped on the spur, heel and toe of Italy's "boot," Campania is emerging as having the most potential.

In the Glass

With vineyards covering virtually every acre of Italy, it's no wonder that many people find navigating Italian wine difficult. But once you know the four basic areas and the four label designations, the experimentation can begin. Ask the local wine merchant to provide some inexpensive recommendations for each area, then find a few favorites and splurge.

In Piedmont, the best known wine pioneer is fourth-generation Angelo Gaja, whose great grandfather founded the winery in 1859. Though tradition runs deep in his family, Gaja embraced new winemaking techniques in the 1970s, such as single-vineyard wines and oak barrel aging, that led to world-renown for Barbaresco. He's known for being a savvy marketer, as well as a passionate businessman — and it shows in the wine. Gaja Barbaresco, particularly the Sori Tildin single-vineyard label, is well balanced, complex, and is fairly bursting with silky tannins and chocolate and fig flavors. Good vintages can last for decades in a cellar, so expect to pay a hefty price — anywhere from $250 to $350 — for this treasure. Other Barbaresco producers to look for include Marchesi di Gresy, Pelissero, and Produttori del Barbaresco. Just keep in mind that these wines are almost always obtained at a premium.

Bruno and Marcello Ceretto, often called the Barolo Brothers, took over their father's wine business in the 1960s and quickly have established their labels as offering quality and value. The best Barolo the brothers create is the Bricco Rocche, which is only bottled in the finest vintages, making it the most expensive of their three Barolos. But if the more than $200 price tag of Bricco Rocche is too high, try Ceretto's Brunate Barolo, which is usually a little more than $100, or Prapo Barolo, which is usually in the $80 range. In general, Barolo, has a much higher production year to year, so the prices shouldn't be quite as shocking as Barbaresco. Other producers to look for include Poderi Luigi Einaudi, Elio Altare, Vietti, and Bartolo Mascarello.

When it comes to Italian whites, Friuli-Venezia Giulia represents the country's heart. And no other Friuli winemaker has done more to give the region personality than Silvio Jermann. At just 21 years old, Jermann creatively blended chardonnay, sauvignon blanc and ribolla gialla to make Vintage Tunina, which started Friuli's trend in blending whites. He went on to continually coerce balanced, powerful flavors from white grapes — and give the blends quirky names, such as the barrel-fermented chardonnay Where the Dreams Have No End, to attract attention. But the wine that started it all remains one of his best and can be found for around $50. Other producers to look for include Abbazia di Rosazzo, Schiopetto, Steverjan, Venica & Venica and Marco Felluga.

As the northernmost grape-growing region in Italy, the varied microclimates of Alto Adige are known for producing interesting reds and crisp white wines, particularly those of Alois Lageder. A native to the region, Lageder has spent his winemaking career focused on sustainable organic farming whenever possible, and even built a low-energy-consumption office building at his Tor Lowengang winery. Careful attention to detail in selecting fruit and modern winemaking technology result in wines with bracing acidity and mineral flavors. Legeder offers three different levels of wines, including classic, vineyard selection, and flagship estate wines, but classic offers an inexpensive entrance into some of Alto Adige's best-tasting bottles. Lageder's Pinot Bianco is a fruity, clean-tasting wine that runs a very reasonable $12-$15 a bottle. Other producers to look for include J. Hofstatter and Tiefenbrunner.

Taking chances has helped Italy's winemakers revive the industry, and no one embodies this spirited approach more than Piero Antinori. Inspired by Italy's first cabernet sauvignon, Sassicaia, Antinori was at the forefront of pushing Tuscany's quality up by abandoning long-held traditions in Chianti. Despite the naysayers, Antinori made Tignanello, a proprietary blend of sangiovese, cabernet sauvignon and cabernet franc — one of the first wines to eschew Chianti's original recipe, which called for a blend of white and red grapes. The resulting wine ($75-$85) is a consistent favorite, with soft tannins and rich fruit flavors. Other labels to look for include Ornellaia, Marchesi Incisa della Rochetta, Poggio Antico, Ruffino, Volpaia and Monsanto.

Italy

Chapter 8
Spain

When wine explorers talk about discovering new regions and vintages, they're generally referring to the wines of the New World, with one important exception. Though Spain borders the very heart of the Old World wine industry, France, it's only been in the last few decades that Spanish wines have begun frequently making their way to American goblets — mostly because the quality was spotty and even the good wines tended to age in barrels for too long by most standards. And while these days connoisseurs are fluent in regions such as Rioja and Ribera del Duero, emerging areas such as Rias Baixas are attracting the attention of bargain hunters and adventurous drinkers alike.

History

Spain's wine industry has only just begun showing the world what it has to offer, but its history follows a path similar to the rest of Europe. Mediterranean traders established a port in modern-day Cadiz that served as hub for the whole region. Consequently, wine and other commodities made their way into the city, with migrants eventually planting their own vines in the area and winemaking beginning around the middle of the first century A.D.

Political turmoil hindered Spain's wine production off and on for centuries, while phylloxera took its toll in the late 19th and early 20th century. Although the country had established an appellation system in 1932, the Spanish Civil War raged from 1936-1938, further setting the industry back. It wasn't until the 1950s that all of the pieces fell into place and enabled the industry to begin moving forward. Established wineries began upgrading their equipment and techniques, and by the 1970s, Spain had shed its reputation as a plonk producer.

Closely mirroring France's classification methods, the Denominacion de Origen appellation system that Spain introduced in the 1930s was revised once the industry was back on its feet in 1970. (Incidentally, the DO system is also used to certify Spain's indigenous foodstuffs, such as cheese and ham.) There are close to 60 DO regions in Spain, each of which must follow fairly strict guidelines from the National Institute of Denominations of Origin that dictate quality control. A laboratory and tasting panel certifies every wine that has DO status.

In addition to the DO designation that appears on Spanish wine labels, the country has introduced a handful of more specific designations since the 1970s. DOCa, which stands for Denominacion de Origen Calificada, applies only to wines from Rioja and Priorato and is used to indicate wines that have a long history of high quality. New legislation provided high-quality estates, regardless of their DO status, with the new Denominacion de Origen de Pago Calificada designation, which appeared in 2003 and is geared toward recognizing specific terroir. And for wines that have yet to achieve DO status but are a step above table wine, the Vino de Calidad con Indicacion Geografica (VCIG) designation appears on the label.

Ports of Call

Rich fortified wines characterize Portugal

Sharing the Iberian peninsula with Spain, Portugal is best known for its succulent, fleshy port, a fortified wine that originates in the Port region along the Douro River (known as the Duero in Spain). But these days, dry table wine is becoming as much a part of Portuguese heritage as its sweet cousin.

Almost all port begins with the same initial process of maceration and fermentation, but at the point when about half of the grapes' sugar has turned to alcohol, clear high-proof brandy is added. The brandy kills off the yeast, which ends fermentation, resulting in a wine with about 10% residual sugar and 20% alcohol. From there, the aging determines what style the port will be. Although there are 10 different resulting styles, knowing the three majors eliminates most of the confusion. Ruby port has next to no aging before it's released, and it's generally the least expensive. Tawny port can be young or aged, but the aged variety is the tastiest. It's made from port left in the barrel until it has a brownish color and takes on the woody, caramel flavors of its surroundings. And, finally, vintage port, which has a year on the label, is the highest echelon — meaning it's the most expensive and the most highly sought after.

Portugal produces another fortified wine in its island province of Madeira, which takes the name of its area. Madeira is made in much the same way as port, but it is heated during the barrel-aging process. For the very best Madeiras, this means that the barrels are stored in hot attics for up to 20 years before bottling. Exceptional nut and caramel flavors, with enough acidity to avoid being overly sweet, are a revelation for anyone who's never tried one.

While labor-intensive fortified wine remains intrinsic to Portugal's industry, the country is also focusing on inexpensive table wine, which take on the name of their region. For wine of higher quality, the term garrafeira appears on the label, indicating that a red wine has been aged for two years before bottling and a white wine has been aged six months before bottling and six months in the bottle. Major sources for drinkable bargains include the Minho, which makes the refreshing white wine Vinjo Verde; Douro, which produces excellent red; Dao, known for red; and Bairrada, which makes a lot of sparkling wine.

The Regions

With Americans' demand for Spanish wines increasing each year, it's no wonder that importers are constantly seeking out new sources. But although regions like Campo de Borja, Navarra, Rueda and Bierzo are producing reasonably-priced vintages that are exciting wine drinkers across the U.S., Spain's five better-known major regions — Rioja, Ribera del Duero, Rias Baixas, Jerez and Penedes— remain the most consistent in quality.

Red wine dominates in Spain's Rioja region, which has been the country's premiere winemaking area for more than 100 years. Tracing much of its viticultural heritage back to France, Rioja actually became a French winemaking outpost of sorts in the 19th century. At that time, Bordeaux was riddled with vineyard diseases that led to wine shortages, so many Bordelaise traveled south hoping to replant and rebuild. While the boom in Rioja was cut short by phylloxera, the French influence remains.

Although Rioja is less than an hour from water, its surrounding mountains shield it from any maritime influence, as well as keep the often-wild winds at bay. Like its winemaking compadres in Bordeaux, Rioja produces blended wine — which is mostly made from the tempranillo grape with smaller portions of grenache (called garnacha in Spain), carignan (known as mazuelo in Spain) and graciano mixed in — known for its signature dense, earthy, berry qualities. The blends are oak-barrel aged — another signature practice Rioja winemakers learned from the French — often for much longer than most other wines in the world. In fact, prior to Spain's viticultural renaissance in the 1950s and 1960s, some wines were aged for decades, resulting in a vintage stripped of its characteristic fruit flavors.

Several terms indicating a wine's aging time and grape quality appear on bottles originating in Rioja. (These terms don't always appear on the front label, but they will be listed on the official government stamp on the neck of the bottle.) "Vino joven" or "sin crianza" means the wine has less than six months in oak barrels or no aging at all and has been made with lower-quality grapes. "Crianza" on a white wine requires six months in oak; for red wine, the vintage must age for two years, with one of those years spent in oak barrels. Made from good-quality grapes, crianza wines are inexpensive and very drinkable. "Reserva" white wine has spent at least six months in oak and six months in the bottle; red reservas usually have a year in oak and two years in the bottle. These are made from exceptional-quality grapes and are usually only bottled in good harvest years. And the most rare, "gran reserva, " indicates a white wine that has spent six months in oak and more than three years in the bottle; red gran reservas generally have two years in oak and three years in the bottle, though some spend as much as eight years aging before release.

As in Rioja, the Castile and Leon province's Ribera del Duero produces wine that ages much longer than most, which are noted on the bottle by the same terms. The Duero takes its name from the gentle river that flows through the valley, but this harsh region is known for extreme temperature changes throughout any given day during the summer, perhaps contributing to the wine's rustic, wild characteristics. Although the tinta fino grapes grown in the region are related to Rioja's tempranillo, Ribera del Duero's vintages tend to be more boldly flavored with a heavier texture. In fact, while Rioja's French influence gives it cachet in the wine world, many connoisseurs consider a handful of labels from the Duero to be some of the most exquisite wine the world has to offer.

Red wine dominates Spain's wine production, but the Rias Baixas region is changing perceptions about Spanish wine by producing heralded white wine made from the albarino grape. Rias Baixas benefits from a cool Atlantic Ocean breeze, making it ideal for white grape-growing. Albarino from this region generally has a lot of zesty citrus flavor, as well as creamy vanilla, peach and honey scents. Unlike the rest of Spain, Rias Baixas labels its wine by grape rather than region, making it simple to find in the wine store.

Another discovery in the last decade for the wine intelligensia is the Catalonia province's Priorato, whose wines started taking educated palates by surprise in the 1990s. Vineyards were probably planted here even before the Roman Empire, and many of the grenache and carignan vines are extremely old, which means the wine produced from their fruit has concentrated flavors, good structure and dark tannins. Sharing the exclusive DOCa designation with Rioja means that Priorat wines don't come cheap, so be sure to get a recommendation from a wine merchant to make splurging a success.

Jerez, which is in the southern part of the Andalusia province, is known exclusively for its sherry. While most Americans associate this fortified wine with the cheap stuff for cooking, sherry is a part of everyday life in Spain, and its flavor can be bone-dry to extremely sweet. Most sherries are made from the white palomino grape and fall into two categories: fino, which tend to be lighter and tangier, and oloroso, which are heavy and dark. Like all other wines, the flavors and texture vary with each producer, so ask for a recommendation based on preferred sweetness and style.

Like Jerez, Penedes is known mostly for one style of wine, sparkling. Cava is Spain's version of sparkling wine and is made using France's Champagne method, with wine from parellada, macabeo, xarel-lo and, increasingly, chardonnay grapes. Only sparkling wine made in this region using the French method can be called cava on the label. As with Champagne, the sweetness varies from brut, which has virtually no residual sugar, to demi-sec (semiseco in Spanish), which is rather sweet.

In the Glass

Although the world is finally uncorking bottles from Spain, the country's grape vines never knew that no one was watching. Their gnarled trunks continued producing grapes unabated, growing ever more tangled with each passing season. And now that the spotlight has returned, wine producers such as Emilio Moro are reaping the benefits. Named for the winery's founder, who was born in 1933 in the Pesquera winemaking region and grew up stomping grapes alongside his father, Emilio Moro crafts wine from tempranillo vines that are up to 80 years old. The resulting Ribero del Duero wine, called Malleolus, is powerful in color and flavor, with dark fruit and spicy oak on the palate. Expect to pay about $80 for a bottle, but think of it as history in a glass. Other labels to look for include Alvaro Palacio, Coto de Hayas, Marques de Murrieta, Marques de Caceres, Cune, Pesquera, Torres and Vega Sicilia.

Chapter 9

Germany

Despite Germany's reputation for sweet dessert-style wines, this cool northern country is a haven for wine drinkers who like dry, crisp vintages with mineral notes — a refreshing change from more popular oaky chardonnay. While German wine has been unfashionable for more than three decades, in-the-know connoisseurs consider Germany's reisling to be the best interpretation of the grape in the world. And although the gothic-scripted labels can look confusing someone who doesn't speak German, they're really chock-full of information that a well-informed novice can use to choose precisely the right bottle for an evening. On the other hand, Germany is known for having the most complicated labels in the wine world, so if all else fails, the friendly neighborhood wine merchant can offer assistance.

The History

With a winemaking history that has been traced back to the days when the Romans rules the European continent, Germany is one of the oldest of the Old World wine regions. In the 19th and early 20th century, Germany was second only to France in its reputation for producing preeminent wine, including its coveted and extremely expensive sweet dessert-style vintages, beerenauslese and trockenbeerenauslese. But much like the rest of the established wine world, the two world wars — during which time some of the country's leading wine exporters faced anti-Semitism — and social hardship dealt a difficult blow to the German wine industry.

In the 1950s, the industry bounced back and made a concerted effort to bring order to its somewhat discombobulated system of vineyards and introduce new grapes. Unfortunately, the reorganized did little to focus on elevating quality; instead it called for vineyards to be planted in areas that were easy to harvest, rather than the steep hillsides that allowed for better fruit. Decades of misguided attempts at reform culminated with a 1971 law that was supposed to simplify German wine. Though the law still serves as the basis of classification today, it's based on the ripeness of grapes at harvest, which doesn't indicate the quality of the wine. Needless to say, it remains a sore spot for top-quality producers.

The 1971 law established the country's 11 regions (two more were added in 1989 when Germany's two halves were reunited) and divided German wines into three basic classifications. The highest level of these is Qualitatswein mit Pradikat (QmP), which constitutes about 95% of the wine made in the country. The main characteristic of a QmP wine is that it cannot by law be chaptalized, which is a process that winemakers use to boost the alcohol content. (It's somewhat common in France and entails adding more sugar for the yeast to consume, which doesn't alter the sweetness.) QmP wines are further divided into six sub-categories that indicate the degree of ripeness of the grape: Auslese wine is made from very ripe hand-selected grape bunches, which means they're usually sweet and expensive; the rare and pricy beerenauslese (called B.A. for brevity's sake) is late-harvest and made from grapes that have botrytisized so the flavors are concentrated; eiswein, or ice wine, is made from ripened grapes that have frozen on the vine to concentrate the juice; trockenbeerenauslese (usually shortened to T.B.A.) is only made in the best years, requires hand-harvesting and is outrageously expensive; kabinett is low-alcohol, food-friendly and dry — it's usually the lightest in body of QmP wines; spatlese, made from very ripe grapes, usually has a pleasant acidity and can be dry or sweet.

A step below QmP is Qualitatswein bestimmter Aubaugebiete (QbA), which denotes wine that comes from one of Germany's 13 designated winegrowing regions. Chaptalization is acceptable for these everyday drinking wines. And at the bottom of the hierarchy are tafelwein, or table wine, and landwein. Neither one of these inexpensive, neutral tasting types usually make it to stores in the United States, and very little of the country's wine production receives these classifications.

Two other terms that are common on a German label are trocken, which means dry, and halbtrocken, which means half-dry. Because of Germany's cold climate, even wines that are labeled halbtrocken usually have a high enough acid content to ameliorate any sweetness that would otherwise taste cloying. Beginning in 2000, some German wines eschewed the old trocken-halbtrocken designation for the terms classic and selection. Classic indicates a dry wine, selection is a wine with 1.2% residual sugar — and when neither term appears, it's usually a somewhat sweet wine.

Some areas have taken the initiative to develop their own regional/varietal wines with decidedly uncomplicated labels. The winemakers in the region usually decide on a type of wine to make, then design an easy-to-read label that all producers use, only listing the region and the grape varietal.

There's also a German organization called Verband Deutscher Prädikats or VDP for short, which consists of 200 wineries dedicated to producing high-quality wine. In 2002, VDP decided on a classification system that's similar to France's grand cru and is noted directly on the label with a logo depicting a grape bunch on the breast of an eagle.

The Regions

Within Germany's baker's dozen of recognized wine regions are four that are renowned for their quality: the Mosel-Saar-Ruwer, the Rheingau, the Pfalz and the Rheinhessen.

Named for a river that flows into the Rhine, the Mosel is characterized by its extremely steep vineyards and cold climate (Saar and Ruwer are even colder tributaries to the Mosel River that are a part of the wine region). Compared to other wine regions in the world, the Mosel receives a minimal amount of sunlight, which means that in order for the grapes to ripen at all, the vines have to be in precisely the right spot for maximum exposure. Most of the best wineries concentrated in the middle of the region in villages such as Bernkastel, Piesport and Wehlen. As with the rest of the country, reisling is the dominant grape, with some muller-thurgau and elbling rounding out production. Because of the difficult climate, vintages are important in Mosel, but in good years, the bottles age well and offer a fresh, delicately flavored treasure. Incidentally, the easiest way to discern a wine from Mosel is its typical green bottle; Rhein wines are packaged in brown bottles.

Like so much of the rest of Europe's wine regions, the Rheingau is steeped in tradition — but that doesn't mean its winemakers are averse to change. With the wines of Mosel and the Pfalz challenging the Rheingau's status as Germany's top region, the Rheingau introduced a vineyard-classification system called erstes gewachs, which was introduced into law ahead of the VDP's 2002 classification. In order to qualify, a vineyard must only cultivate reisling and spatburgunder grapes, and the wine itself has to meet a specific standard. Unlike the wine of Mosel, the Rheingau produces fruitier, richer reisling, and some other grapes are starting to take hold such as pinot blanc (known as weissburgunder), chardonnay and even the red grape pinot noir, which goes by its German name, spatburgunder.

The Rheinhessen is Germany's largest wine region, and it's mostly known for inexpensive Liebfraumilch, a generic table wine that frequently makes its way to the United States. But there are a few top producers in the region that make earthy reislings, and the regional wine Rheinhessen sylvaner is a dry QbA worth checking out.

Although the Pfalz is in the Rhine Valley, it has a more southerly climate that gives its wine a fruitier, creamier character than its fellow regions. Reisling still dominates, but the sunny weather gives gewurtztraminer, pinot blanc, pinot gris (in German, it's called rulander), and pinot noir good growing conditions, too. Most of Pfalz wines are good for everyday drinking.

Among the other regions gaining notoriety are Ahr, Baden, Nahe, Mittelrhein and Franken.

The World Wine Encyclopedia

In the Glass

With a confusing system of laws and labeling, German can confound even the savviest of wine drinkers. But anyone who has tackled the task of learning about an unfamiliar wine region knows that it's easier to learn bottle by bottle than by memorizing villages and producers. And after a few good recommendations from a wine store, even a novice should be well on the way to cutting through the clutter of German wine labels.

While most wineries in the United States boast a history that goes back a few decades, German wineries tend to reach back several centuries to point to their beginnings. For example, the Prum family in the Mosel has been cultivating vines in the villages of Bernkastel, Graach, Wehlen and Zeltigen since 1156, but the "modern era" began in 1842, when Jodocus Prum constructed sundials in Wehlen and Zeltigen. Although the sundials were erected to help the vineyard workers know when to stop for lunch, they've become a historical part of the area and now denote some of the best grape-growing areas in the region. S.A. Prum winery, which features the sundial right on the label, is still operated by a descendant of Jodocus, Raimond Prum, who has been managing the winery for more than three decades. With help from his wife and children, Raimond has built S.A. Prum's reputation for top-quality estate bottled reisling and pinot blanc. In addition, the winery is a founding member of VDP. Other producers in the Mosel to look for include Dr. Loosen, Schloss Saarstein, Selbach-Oster, Fritz Haag, Reichsgraf von Kesselstatt and Reinhold Haart.

For more than a century, the Breuer family has been cultivating vines along the steep banks of the Rhine River in the Rheingau and earning a reputation for making some of the best reisling in the area. But while the Georg Breuer label comes from the heart of Germany, it looks more like a postcard from an art museum. In place of the usual heavy script and the many traditional designations is commissioned artwork from artists working all over the world — a tradition the George Breuer winery has been carrying on for more than 20 years. Other producers in the Rheingau to look for include August Eser, Franz Kunstler, Josef Leitz and Johannishof.

Chapter 10

Austria

Despite having a culture and language that overlaps with Germany, Austria has a climate that provides it with much more flexibility in winemaking than its neighbor to the west. And although, as in Germany, the majority of grapes planted in Austria are white, this Central European country is taking advantage of its warmer weather and creating exciting pinot noir and cabernet sauvignon. Its wine exports are still mostly going to Germany, the Czech Republic and Italy, but Americans are starting to take note of this emerging international wine region.

History

The ancient Celts introduced winemaking to Austria in about 1000 BC, and viticulture thrived into the fifth century AD when the Roman Empire reigned. As in much of the rest of Europe, winemaking became the domain of monks during the Middle Ages; they settled in the eastern part of Austria, and used wine for religious ceremonies. In the subsequent centuries, viticulture became an increasingly important part of the region.

When Austria became its own country in 1919, it had already established several viticultural schools, and by the end of World War II had adopted an appellation system similar to that of Germany. Unfortunately, the still-unstable country was forced to make cheap, sweet wine to pay the bills, and wineries cut corners wherever possible. The industry hit an all-time low in 1985 when a small group of wine brokers was caught adding antifreeze to low-quality wines to make it taste sweeter, and to pass them off as more expensive vintages. Luckily, no one died following the scandal, and it led Austria to make immediate, sweeping changes in its wine industry — starting with the Wine Law of 1985.

Austrian wine is still difficult to find in the United States, but successful seekers will discover that its labels looks very similar to German wine. For obvious reasons, Austria's wine laws are the strictest in Europe, and are based on the grapes' sugar level at harvest. The various levels can indicate quality, but they don't necessarily guarantee it. If a wine merchant carries Austrian vintages, it's likely he or she can steer a curious consumer to a great bottle. (See chapter 9 for specific levels of classification.)

Bottled Up

They might not be major producers, but these European countries are happy to crush grapes.

Although tasting wine from around the world is the easiest way to get to know a country without traveling, some regions require a visit to sample the local wares. While Switzerland, England and Wales produce wine, most of it never travels very far outside of country borders.

Switzerland loves the red wine of Burgundy and Beaujolais, so a third of the vines in the Valais region are pinot noir and gamay, which are usually blended together to create a light, fruity wine. Not surprisingly, most of the country's wine comes from the areas where French is the dominant language. However, the Swiss consume most of what they produce, so the bottles that make it to other countries are expensive.

Tourists and locals are usually the only ones quaffing the wines of England and Wales, too. Despite a climate that's decidedly dark for grape growing, these two countries have about 2,000 acres planted, with most of the vines yielding white grapes. Cold-climate grapes grow the best, including such varietals as muller-thurgau, seyval blanc and bacchus on the white side, and dornfelder on the red. Unfortunately, these wines tend to be quite expensive when they make it to America, so bargain hunters beware.

Regions

Since monks from Burgundy and Bavaria first began making wine in Austria, all of the country's four major regions fall along the eastern border with Hungary and Slovakia. The largest area, Lower Austria (known as Niederosterreich), accounts for a little more than 90% of the country's wine production and comprises five districts, including Wachau, which borders the Danube River and is known for crisp, peppery white gruner veltliner, as well as full-bodied reisling. Incidentally, Wachau is the only region in Austria that doesn't classify its wine based on the ripeness of the grapes. Instead, the terms steinfeder (no added sugar, or chaptalization, and no more than 10.7% alcohol), federspiel (no chaptalization and no more than 11.9% alcohol) and smaragd (considered the best Austrian wines, with a minimum of 11.3% alcohol) appear on the label.

Although Vienna resides in the middle of Lower Austria, it is classified as its own distinct region. Known as Wein in Austria, Vienna has a unique tradition in which it merges its wineries with sidewalk cafés called heurigen. Heurigen are always attached to a vineyard that produces all of the wine served in the establishment; patrons come to chat, hear music, snack and drink in a casual atmosphere. Reisling rules the vineyards here, but there are some plantings of pinot blanc and chardonnay, as well as red zweigelt and cabernet sauvignon.

Burgenland, which was a part of Hungary until 1921, is known for its dessert-style wines, most notably ausbruch. The grapes are left on the vine after they're ripe, and botrytis (or "noble rot") concentrates the sugars, in the same way a French Sauternes is made. The nearby Neusiedl Lake keeps the temperature moderate and the humidity at just the right level to encourage botrytis. Burgenland also makes German-style beerenauslese, trockenbeerenauslese and eiswein from welschreisling, pinot blanc, neuberger and chardonnay grapes. Red wine production remains in the minority, but the local grapes of blaufrankisch (also known as lemberger), zweigelt and St. Laurent make some appealing vintages.

Just west of Burgenland, Styria is a cooler Alpine region that's known for mineral, acidic sauvignon blanc and chardonnay (called morillon here). In addition, Styria produces a type of rosé called schilcher from the blauer wildbacher grape.

In the Glass

With grapes like chardonnay and cabernet sauvignon becoming dominant around the world, maintaining vines of less well-known varietals becomes difficult for many producers. But for Wachau's F.X. Pilcher, selecting only the best clones of gruner veltliner has been the family business for close to a century. Beginning in 1928, F.X. Pilcher Sr. kept scrupulous records on the vines in his fields, focusing on the ones with smaller grapes and lower yields. Now in its fifth generation, the family winery is among the best known in Lower Austria, renowned for gruner veltliner with ripe apricot and peach flavors complemented by peppery notes. This label is tough to find in the U.S., but worth investigating. Other labels to look for include J. Hick, Brundlmayer, Hirtzberger and Bernhard Ott.

Chapter 11
Greece

Although thoughts of Greece usually conjure pristine beaches and sun-seeking tourists, the prevailing wisdom doesn't entirely hold true when it comes to pinning down the country's climate. While the warm Mediterranean weather so friendly to grape growing represents a part of what Greece offers viticulture, this starting point of western civilization shares the complex climates that typify its neighbor to the west, Italy. Greece's growing conditions present a wide array, from hot and arid to cool and alpine, which is probably why wine has been made on this land since Hippocrates and Aristotle wrote of its virtues. More importantly, Greek wine is not just about pine-flavored retsina anymore.

The History

The first attempts at winemaking in ancient Greece remain undocumented, but many experts trace it back to somewhere around 2500 B.C. to one of the country's earliest civilizations, the Minoans, who had an active trading tradition with Egypt and other eastern cultures. Later, the Greeks' thirst for colonization in Europe, Africa and Asia helped the wine tradition spread throughout the region. Ancient Greece is also thought to have pioneered the first appellation system before the first millennium A.D. to ensure the authenticity of the wine exported to other areas. By all accounts, the Greeks laid the foundation for viticulture that serves as the basis of today's modern industry.

Although Greece reigned supreme in the wine of the ancient world, its current status in the industry gives little hint of its former glory. From the time that the Ottoman Empire took over Greece around the 15th century, the country's wine production has been hampered by political turmoil, disease and a lack of development. However, since the 1980s, Greece has been poised to build on its heritage, with an eye toward quality.

Much like the rest of the wine world, Greece in the 1970s was a time when vintners began pushing to elevate the prestige and excellence of its wine. Although the Greek Ministry of Agriculture passed a series of laws in 1971 to govern the wine community, Greece adopted an appellation system that's similar to that of France when it joined the European Economic Community in the 1980s.

There are three basic levels within the Greek appellation system. The first and most important level is Appellation of Origin of Superior Quality, which is usually shortened to its Greek acronym, OPAP. The wines in this category are dry, come from one of the 25 recognized appellations and follow specific methods of winemaking. (Sweet wines are denoted by Controlled Appellations of Origin, which is shortened to OPE. There are seven recognized OPE regions.) Both OPAP and OPE wines can also have two other designations on the label, reserve and grand reserve, both of which indicate that the wines have been barrel aged. The other two levels, Topikos Oenos and Epitrapezios Oenos, have less stringent guidelines when it comes to regions and grapes.

While all three designations do indicate a wine of Greek descent, the level of quality is dictated by the final product — a skilled wine merchant can help guide a novice to the best that the country has to offer. The labels can be confusing because producers name the wines based on the region (usually for the most prestigious), by varietal or, occasionally, even by a proprietary name. However, even without the help of a professional, it's tough to make a mistake that's expensive: Most of the country's bottles cost about $10, with higher quality vintages hovering around $20.

Greece

Global Warming

Just about every country with halfway decent growing conditions is cozying up to wine production.

While California and France continue to set the trends for the wine world, vintages do not begin and end with the major regions. In whatever corner of the world that grape vines can grow, there's usually an entrepreneurial vintner hoping to use the fruit to make palatable wine.

And nowhere is this more apparent than in Eastern Europe. Since Communism released its hold on the region in 1989, the world is beginning to realize that decent vintages can come from all over the continent. Leading the charge with more than 20 recognized regions is Hungary, whose only export for decades was the dessert wine Tokay. The dry red wine for which it's gaining global fans used to be only known to citizens behind the Iron Curtain.

In addition to Hungary, wines from the Czech Republic, Romania, the Western Balkans, Bulgaria, Turkey and Israel are also making their way to market with reasonable prices to encourage the curious.

Even the Asian continent is seeing wine production these days. Despite the prevalence of rice wine, several northeastern provinces in China are growing chardonnay, while Japan is experimenting with Bordeaux-style blends and India is producing sparkling wine.

The Regions

With the seas of the Mediterranean, Aegean and Ionian surrounding the Greek mainland and its thousands of tiny islands, the country has a relatively small amount of land suitable for agriculture.. Nevertheless, planted among the olive trees and grazing livestock are vineyards devoted to native and imported grape varieties, which enjoy a climate with plenty of sun and the benefit of a maritime influence. And like their Italian neighbors, the Greeks are creating unique wine styles by blending native grapes with chardonnay, merlot and cabernet sauvignon. Although more than three-quarters of Greece's wine production is white, exotic-sounding indigenous red grapes such as xynomavro, agiorgitiko and kotsifali make bold vintages that are gaining attention.

Although there are many small regions scattered all over Greece, there are fewer than a half-dozen that stand out among wine aficionados. The most notable region is Naoussa, which is in Macedonia and produces some of the country's best wine made from xynomavro, which creates a deep-red, rich elixir. The southern mainland, called Peloponnese, has three regions of note: Nemea, Mantinia and Patrias. Of these, Nemea is gaining the most notice in the last five years because of its lush, peppery wine made from agiorgitiko, which is considered among the best winemaking grapes in Greece. The Aegean Island of Santorini is famous for its spectacular vistas and its mild, food-friendly white wine made from assyrtiko grapes, as well as its visanto, a barrel-aged, dessert-style wine made. And Crete has some of its own native grapes, including kotsifali and mandelari, which are crucial to making wine in the island's most notable region, Archarnes.

In the Glass

Outside of authentic Greek restaurants, the wines of Greece usually are given little more than a shelf in U.S. wines stores. But inquiring imbibers will almost always be able to find one authentic Greek label at both eating establishments and wine shops: Boutari. When John Boutaris founded the original winery at Naoussa in 1879, the wine Boutari released was somewhat of a novelty at the time, but it was tremendously successful and the label grew to become synonymous with the Greek wine industry. Even today, Boutari Naoussa Grand Reserve is among the most highly regarded wines that Greece produces. In addition, the company is still family-run: Its chairman is Constantine Boutaris, whose daughter Marina is its director of communications and represents the fifth generation to take the reins. Other labels to look for include Gaia Estate, Kostas Lazaridis, Skouras, Harlaftis and Pape Johannou.

Chapter 12

Australia & New Zealand

Breaking the rules is where the excitement surrounding New World wines lies. Though countries like Australia and New Zealand don't have centuries of winemaking tradition from which to draw knowledge, they also aren't hampered by institutionalized regulations and systems. And the rest of the world is catching on to what the United Kingdom — the largest importer of Australian and New Zealander wine — has known for at least a few decades: This part of the Southern Hemisphere offers reasonably priced fruit-forward reds and concentrated whites.

The History

Compared with Old World regions, both countries have a relatively short history of cultivating vineyards, and making wine from the fruit really began taking hold in the last 100 years.

Australia made its first forays into wine in the early 19th century, when Scotsman James Busby immigrated from Bordeaux, where he had been studying winemaking, and started an agricultural school that specialized in viticulture. After using the school's vineyard to make a decent barrel of wine, he began touring wine regions in Spain and France, returning to Australia with more than 500 vine clippings that he then planted in Sydney, as well as Victoria and South Australia. Not all of the vines survived, but Busby helped developed a thriving wine industry that met domestic needs up through the 1950s.

It's no wonder Busby is called the father of the Australian wine industry, but he also played a crucial role in establishing vines in New Zealand, as well as the country's political history. After being designated "Official British Resident" by the British government, Busby arrived in the Bay of Islands, home to the Maori culture, and planted some of the vines he collected in Europe in Waitangi. He made his first wine three years later.

In the 1960s, new viticultural technology enabled Australia to heighten the quality of what its wineries were bottling, and by the 1980s, Australia began exporting its creamy chardonnays to the rest of the world. The country's emphasis on technology has helped it gain a foothold in the wine world in what seems like record time.

New Zealand's industry, which was something of a joke in wine circles up until the 1980s, is gaining in worldwide popularity, but its exports continue to be dwarfed by Australia.

Unlike the wine laws of many other countries, Australia doesn't have the strictly enforced appellations of France or even the simple A.V.A.s of the United States. The only rules winemakers must follow relate to labeling: First, if a region is mentioned on the label, 85 percent of the wine must come from that area. Second, if a certain grape variety is listed on the label, 85 percent of the wine must be made from that grape. And finally, if a wine is a blend, the greater percentage must be listed first. For example, if a wine is 90 percent chardonnay and 10 percent semillon, it would say "Chardonnay-Semillon" on the label.

New Zealand doesn't follow an appellation system, either, though a system of Certified Origin is in the works, which will guarantee that a wine does originate from the country. Its labeling conventions are similar to those of Australia, with blended wines requiring the dominant grape listed first. For grape varieties listed on the label, 75 percent must be the listed grape. If a region is mentioned, 75 percent of the wine must come from that location.

The Regions

Australia

Most wines around the world are discussed in terms of terroir, or what the place where grapes are grown imparts on the wine itself. However, instead of touting the viticulture of a specific hillside with a certain soil type, Australians have found success in creating blends that come from many different areas of the country. In fact, the region of many Aussie wines is listed as Southeast Australia, which incorporates the vast majority of the country's wineries. And while Australian chardonnay is phenomenally popular around the world, close to 60 percent of the wine sold locally is inexpensive "wine in a box," made from grapes as varied as trebbiano, muscat gordo blanco and French columbard.

Though this continent is nearly as large as the United States, almost all of its wineries are found around the less-arid outer edges on the southern part of the country. Six major regions make up Australia's winemaking industry: Western Australia, South Australia, Victoria, New South Wales, Queensland and Tasmania. Because of its emphasis on a national wine identity, the industry has yet to break down these areas into specific terroir. However, several large and small producers are making wine that highlights the best of what the country's soil and vines have to offer.

Producing half of the wine coming out of the country, South Australia is the largest region and home to some of the most recognizable areas for bulk and high-quality Aussie wine. The limestone ridge of Coonawarra, which has built its reputation on structured cabernet sauvignon with lush, full fruit notes, was founded by wine-industry trailblazing labels Penfolds and Lindemanns, while the hot Barossa Valley is making a name for itself with ripe shiraz and reisling, though the really good reisling comes from cooler areas like the Clare Valley and the Adelaide Hills. Most of the mass-market wines come from an irrigated area along the Murray River commonly called Riverland, which uses mechanized harvesting to ratchet up its output.

Second to South Australia in wine production is New South Wales, whose industry is centered on the relatively small Hunter Valley, which is divided into Upper and Lower regions: Mudgee, which is warmer and drier than Hunter Valley; and Riverina, which produces the state's bulk wine. Strangely enough, Hunter Valley offers a less-than-ideal climate for grape growing, with drought in the spring and too much humidity during harvest. Even so, the region has a star chardonnay in Rosemount Estate's Roxburgh, and many patient wine collectors find that after at least five years in the bottle Hunter Valley semillon is a toasty, buttery revelation. Mudgee is better known for its very structured cabernet sauvignon. And although the well-known label Yellowtail hearkens from Riverina, this area also makes some very good semillon-based dessert wines.

Victoria got its start as a wine region back in the mid-19th century during the gold rush, but once the rush faded, phylloxera devastated the grape vines. It wasn't until the 1960s that this area around Melbourne started to turn its wine fortunes around and grape vines were planted in Bendigo, Geelong and the Yarra Valley. Now, more than 200 producers occupy this thriving region, which is best known for the sparkling wines of the district of Grampians and the sweet muscats and tokays of Rutherglen and Glenrowan. Red wines flourish in areas like Bendigo, King Valley, Beechworth and Mornington Peninsula. The Yarra Valley is captivating imbibers with its supple pinot noir, as well as intense shiraz and cabernet.

About 150 miles south of Victoria, the island of Tasmania is relatively new to the wine world, but it's gaining respect for its subtle, more European-style flavors. The weather can be unpredictable, so most producers plant a range of grapes, including chardonnay, reisling, pinot noir and sauvignon blanc. However, the one constant that the area offers is good-quality sparkling wine, made from pinot noir and chardonnay.

Almost 3,000 miles from the rest of the country's wine regions, Western Australia had grape vines long before the southern states, but its remote location hindered the growth of the wine industry. However, these days, now that connoisseurs are able to taste the vintages emanating from this area, they're finding that Western Australia has a variety of cool-climate wines, like reisling, as well as warmer-climate favorites, such as shiraz. Most of the wineries are located around the capitol city of Perth, and of these, Margaret River is perhaps the most famous. Warm Indian Ocean breezes buffet the vines, which include French varietals like cabernet sauvignon, merlot and chardonnay. Another well-known district, the Swan Valley, was this part of the country's first wine region and became famous for producing Houghton's White Burgundy, a powerful, alcoholic wine that was all the rage in Australia for decades. But these days, all eyes are on the cooler Great Southern Region, which is having good luck with reisling, chardonnay, shiraz and pinot noir, as well as Perth Hills and Pemberton.

New Zealand

As the southernmost wine region in the world, the North Island and South Island of New Zealand are very sunny — but that doesn't mean this area is warm. In fact, despite ocean breezes, this isolated country has some of the chilliest grape-growing regions in the world, which could be why it's become known for producing great sauvignon blanc. A long growing season allows the grapes to ripen slowly, resulting in wines with good acidity and crisp flavors, though high rainfall and humidity does present its challenges to grape growers. Slightly less than half of the country's wineries are found on the North Island, which has two important regions: Hawkes Bay and Gisborne. Gisborne, which is close to the international dateline, gets the first sunshine of the day in New Zealand and grows mostly white grapes (in fact, its grape growers have dubbed their region the "chardonnay capitol of New Zealand"!). Hawkes Bay also grows a lot of chardonnay, but cabernet sauvignon, syrah, pinot noir and cabernet franc do well here, too. Other regions on the North Island include Auckland, Wellington, which is building a reputation for wonderful pinot noir, Northland and Walkato.

The South Island boasts the country's largest wine district, Marlborough, which didn't begin growing grapes until 1973 but has quickly become the leading producer of sauvignon blanc. Many consider the sauvignon blanc of Marlborough to be some of the best in the world. Other regions on the South Island include Nelson, Canterbury and Central Otago.

In the Glass

Though the new wine industries of Australia and New Zealand don't have as much of the family tradition and bottling heritage as Old World regions, their relative youth enabled them to build state-of-the-art wineries initially, rather than slowly upgrading as countries like Italy and France continue to do. For that reason, they've been able to catch up in terms of quality in a matter of decades.

In Australia, there's no more recognizable name than Penfolds. Dr. Christopher Rawson Penfold, an English doctor who immigrated to the colony in the mid-1800s, believed so much in the medicinal value of wine that he planted French vine cuttings on the property surrounding the Adelaide Hills cottage, dubbed the Grange, that he shared with his wife. From these humble beginnings, the name Penfolds has come to be inextricably linked to Aussie wine, with reports that by the 1920s half of the bottles produced in the country had Penfolds on the label. These days the label is known for its accessible table wines, as well as its super-premium Grange shiraz, which is highly collectable and cellarable for 20 years or more. The first vintage of Penfolds Grange was bottled in 1951.

While Penfolds has vineyards all over Southern Australia and truly dominates the industry, the family tradition that laid the groundwork for all of the country's winemaking remains a part of Leeuwin Estate in Western Australia. As one of the founding wineries in the Margaret River Valley, Leeuwin has, in a short time, become a leading producer of fine chardonnay. Its Art Series chardonnay, named for the commissioned artists who decorate each vintage's labels, has been called the best white wine to come from Australia, with the 2001 vintage earning a near-perfect 98 points from *Wine Spectator* magazine. Other labels to look for across Australia (outside the ubiquitous Yellow Tail, of course) include Peter Lehmann, Rosemount Estate, Hardys and Petaluma.

If there's one winery in all of New Zealand that can be credited with putting the country's sauvignon blanc on the wine map, it's most likely Cloudy Bay Vineyards. Located in Marlborough on the South Island, Cloudy Bay was founded in 1985 by David Hohnen, who had already built success in Australia's Margaret River with winery Cape Mentelle. With the skill of winemaker Kevin Judd (who is still making wine for the company), Cloudy Bay sauvignon blanc developed a reputation for quality on the international market almost as soon as it was released. Other New Zealand labels to look for include Sacred Hills, Neudorf and Seifried.

Chapter 13
South America

A large portion of the South American continent is suitable for growing grapes, and many countries have been producing wines of varying quality for centuries. Though its wine production began modestly, these days countries like Chile and Argentina are being heralded as exciting sources for bold New World wines. Even Peru, Uruguay and Brazil have thriving industries, though their vintages still aren't as easy to find on the shelves of wine stores in the United States.

The History

The history of winemaking in South America begins with mid-16th century Peru, where Spanish conquistadores and missionaries planted European vines that had been imported to Mexico from Spain. Vines from Peru ultimately made their way to Chile, but the still-ruling monarchs of Spain discouraged winemaking in the new territory and in the early 17th century ruled that no wine could be produced there. However, despite Spain's laws, the churches needed wine for Mass, thus winemaking continued unabated. As European settlers continued migrating into South America, winemaking became a bigger part of the country's agriculture, and the governor of Chile ultimately made a recommendation that the ban on homegrown wines be lifted. Once Chile officially achieved its independence from Spain in 1818, its viticultural heritage began in earnest, despite continued political turmoil throughout the following century.

Although early Spanish influences helped build the wine industry in Chile and Argentina, France's influences are dominant today, partly thanks to a French immigrant named Claude Gay. Gay moved to South America in 1828 to study the ecology of the region, establishing a nursery of plant specimens from around the world, including an extensive selection of grape vines. When phylloxera struck Europe, Gay's vines helped restock vineyards and rebuild Europe's industry. In addition, in an effort to emulate the chateaus of Bordeaux, wealthy Chilean land barons who had tasted the wine of France began importing French vine clippings, as well as French winemakers who had lost their jobs because of the phylloxera epidemic.

For the most part, Argentina and Chile follow region and labeling laws that are similar to the United States. For example, in Chile if a wine label designates a particular region, at least 75% of the wine must be made in that region; the same rule holds for a grape varietal listed on the label or a particular vintage. The only specific law in Argentina related to labeling says that if a grape is listed, at least 80% of the wine must be made from that grape.

Uncharted Territory

Mexico isn't just about tequila anymore.

Mention Mexico's wine production at the next tasting party, and it's likely to elicit quizzical glances. But, yes, Mexico does have a tiny but burgeoning wine industry, most of which is on the Baja Peninsula in the Guadalupe Valley.

Much like the rest of Central and South American, winemaking in Mexico dates back hundreds of years, but it has only been in the last decade that the vintages of the country made it north. Mexican wines are still tough to find in North America, so many adventurous wine enthusiasts have ventured to the country to taste what it has to offer first-hand. However, if that isn't an option, keep an eye out for labels from Casa de Piedra, L.A. Cetto, Domecq and Santo Tomas. All of these wineries are producing surprisingly good syrah, merlot and grenache in the warm, dry Mediterranean-style climate.

The Regions

Wine has been a part of South America for at least a century, but it has only been in the last decade its vintages have been making their way outside of the country. Although Chile has been taking steps toward building a fine wine market, its low-cost, great-tasting exports are what make Chilean bottles so popular in North America. As for Argentina, up until a few years ago most of its local wine ended up being consumed within the country, which is why its bottles remain less prevalent in the U.S.

Chile

Bordered by the Andes Mountains to the east and the Pacific Ocean to west, this long, narrow country enjoys a cool breeze that keeps temperatures moderate enough for winemaking. It is also somewhat cut-off from the rest of the continent, which keeps the vines disease- and pest-free, thus mitigating the need for pesticides. In fact, to this day, neither Chile nor Argentina have experienced a phylloxera outbreak, which many experts attribute to both countries' relative isolation. And unlike countries with a limited water supply like Australia, Chile has the runoff from the Andes to keep the vines irrigated.

More than 20 different types of grapes are grown in the country, but Chile's cabernet sauvignon is generally what wows the critics, while chardonnay, merlot and sauvignon blanc represent the country's everyday bargains. There are five major winemaking regions in Chile: Aconcagua Valley, Casablanca Valley, the Central Valley (which comprises four separate valleys, including Maipo, Rapel, Curicó and Maule) Itata Valley and Bio-Bio Valley. Of these, the most renowned are the central region's Maipo and Casablanca, both of which are in the warmer, northern part. Itata and Bio-Bio are the source of some of the cheapest Chilean wine on the market, but their southern, relatively wet location is more conducive to quantity not quality.

Argentina

Of the world's emerging wine regions, Argentina seems to have the most advantage. Not only does it have centuries of winemaking to its credit, but it's attracting wine-industry investors from France and the United States, who are putting Argentina on the fast track to modernization. Although the country continues growing lesser known grapes like criolla and cereza, it's heeding the call of the international market and beginning to plant more French varietals like cabernet sauvignon, chardonnay, malbec and merlot. Incidentally, while malbec is little more than a blending grape in France's Bordeaux region, in Argentina it produces some of the best wine the country has to offer. Argentina also boasts of its white wines made from torrontes, most likely because the grape doesn't really grow anywhere else in the world.

Of Argentina's half-dozen wine regions, Mendoza, which is east of Buenos Aires, and San Juan, which is hotter and farther north. Mendoza is the undisputed capitol of winemaking in the country, comprising nearly three-quarters of Argentina's total production. It's also the source for most Argentine wine making its way into the United States, the majority of which is dense, lush malbec. San Juan is second in production, although most of the vines are cultivated for quantity and don't produce good wine.

Although most of the wines imported into the United States are from Mendoza, there are several other regions of note in Argentina, including Jujuy, Salta, Catamarca, La Rioja and Rio Negro. Keep an eye out for the wines of these regions in the next few years.

The World Wine Encyclopedia

In the Glass

Chile's winemaking heritage traces back as much to its residents as its immigrants — Casa Lapostolle is a perfect blend of the two. The French Marnier Lapostolle family, of orange liqueur Grand Marnier fame, and the Chilean Rabat family joined forces in 1994 to use French winemaking skills to elicit Chilean terroir. And while the venture is relatively new, Casa Lapostolle is producing wine from old French grape vines that were imported prior to France's late 19th century phylloxera outbreak. Though winery produces cabernet sauvignon, carmenere, syrah and sauvignon blanc, its chardonnay and merlot are the most notable. Other producers in Chile to look for include Montes, Santa Rita, Caliterra, Concha y Toro and Tarapaca.

While South America remains an antidote to overpriced California vintages, both Chile and Argentina nevertheless are beginning to dabble in the high end. The most famous example of this is Bodegas Trapiche's Iscay, which comes from Argentina's Mendoza region. When it was first released in 1999, this 50-50 merlot-malbec blend had a price tag of $50 — or about eight times the cost of most Argentine wine. Heralded for its quality, Iscay was the brainchild of Frenchman Michel Roland, a wine consultant who lends his skill to wineries all over the world. Since then, Bodegas Trapiche has taken other cues from France, including a new line of single-vineyard wines designed to express the terroir of the vines in Mendoza. Other producers in Argentina to look for include Alamos, Bodega y Cavas de Weinert, Felipe Rutini and Bodega Norton.

Chapter 14
South Africa

Political turmoil and crippling sanctions kept South Africa's wine industry out of the global market for virtually all of the 20th century. But after the end of apartheid in 1991, its local winemakers were able to upgrade their equipment and adapt to the global marketplace that had developed during their isolation. Not only are the country's vintages being embraced all over the world, but the face of the industry itself is changing. With the government giving black South Africans greater participation in the economy overall, many young black students are seeing opportunities in viticulture.

History

South Africa's winemaking history dates back to the 17th century, when the Dutch East India Company sent Jan van Riebeeck to Cape Town to establish a colony. In addition to building a fort and a pier to aid the ships on the company's trade route, Riebeeck planted vine cuttings from France that resulted in the continent's first wine. But it wasn't until the first Governor of the Cape, Simon van der Stel, planted vines in Constantia that the industry became firmly entrenched. By the 18th century, the Constantia Valley was yielding a sweet wine for which aristocracy around the world clamored.

However, by the late 19th century, phylloxera had destroyed most of the country's vineyards, and once the devastated vines were replanted, overproduction made wine prices plummet. This led to a key development in South Africa's wine industry: the establishment of cooperatives. The first of these were generally unsuccessful in insulating grape growers from the whims of the market, but with the launch of the Cooperative Wine Growers Association of South Africa in 1918, a new day dawned. This powerful organization known by its Afrikaans initials, KWV, controlled every aspect of the wine industry for almost a century. While it did successfully regulate prices, it also stifled innovation and was not focused on quality. KWV still owns a quarter of the wine exports in South Africa, but its power was significant diminished in 1996 when it went from being a cooperative to a group of private companies. Incidentally, in the last decade, the number of wine estates has grown significantly, while the number of cooperatives remains unchanged, which is indicative of the country's move toward focusing on quality instead of quantity.

The wine laws in South Africa are decidedly uncomplicated — a 1972 law called Wine of Origin established the country's official regions. As far as labeling, if a wine has a grape listed, the wine must contain 75% of that grape; if a wine is listed as estate bottled, the wine can come from more than one piece of land in the same district as long as they have similar "ecological conditions."

The World Wine Encyclopedia

Savannah Miles

A look at the handful of other wine regions on the continent of Africa

Outside of South Africa, wine is a relatively small part of the continent's agriculture. A tiny amount is made in Kenya and Zimbabwe, but none of those vintages generally make it any further than the border. The northern part of the continent, despite being dominated by Muslim countries that eschew alcohol, sees winemaking in Egypt and Libya, which is probably mostly appreciated locally.

But along the Atlas Mountains, in the northern countries of Morocco, Algeria and Tunisia, wine production is a significant part of the culture, despite the influences of Islam. All three countries were French colonies up until the mid 20th century and produced a large portion of wine for the international market. When France left, wine production fell, but the French influence continues to inform their wine, even though the countries have yet to break into the global market. In fact, many of Algeria's vineyards are close to 50 years old, and they grow several French varietals, including cinsault, mourvedre and cabernet sauvignon.

Regions

Most of South Africa's wineries are concentrated in the Western Cape's coastline, which offers a more moderate climate than the inland desert regions. Although there are more than a dozen Wine of Origin regions, the Coastal Region — including Constantia, Paarl and Stellenbosch — represents the most recognized. The Coastal Region comprises the areas surrounding Cape Town, whose warm, Mediterranean-style climate is moderated by cooler breezes from the Atlantic and Indian Oceans. The hot inland regions tend to focus more on sweet, dessert-style wines.

Constantia, the site of Simon van der Stel's first vineyard, is somewhat cool for this desert-driven country, with most of its grape vines on high slopes sheltered from the heat by the shadow of the Table Mountains surrounding Cape Town. Stellenbosch, which is home to the country's premier university with a viticulture program, offers a solid mix of historic and modern wineries. And Paarl, which includes the French-influenced Franschhoek Valley, is somewhat warmer and focuses mainly on red wine.

Though the wine produced in South Africa is predominantly white, the vintages causing critics around the world to take notice are red. Cabernet sauvignon, merlot, syrah (which, as in Australia, is called shiraz), and the indigenous grape pinotage, which is a hybrid of pinot noir and cinsault, are the basis for some of the country's most exciting wines. When it comes to white wine, chenin blanc represents the majority of grapes grown, although the internationally popular chardonnay is becoming a bigger part of South Africa's viticulture. Sauvignon blanc, cape riesling and muscadel are also significant parts of its white wine production. The hot inland regions tend to focus more on sweet, dessert-style wines.

Other up-and-coming wine regions in South Africa include Mossel Bay, which is on the Indian Ocean side of the country, Walker Bay and Elgin.

The World Wine Encyclopedia

In the Glass

In just over a decade, the South African wine industry has undergone tremendous change, but nowhere is this more apparent than in the kinds of people crafting what's in the bottle. Indaba wines, the country's fastest-selling label in the United States, could be credited with helping to change the stereotype of the traditional white winemaker. By offering a scholarship to black South Africans interested in pursuing a winemaking career, Indaba educated the first black winemaker in the country's history: Mzokhona Mvemve, who now works as Indaba's official winemaker. Not only was Mvemve the first recipient of the Indaba scholarship, but he has become the preeminent Zulu vintner in the country, with a handful of others following in his footsteps. Other producers to look for include Boschendal, Neil Ellis, Warwick Estate, Meerlust, Kanonkop and Fairview.

Quick Glossary

Definitions for the terms used throughout this
book, as well as common wine terms

Acid: A key element in the structure of a wine. Acid is what makes the mouth water and gives the wine the ability to age well.

Aging: Most wines go through two types of aging: barrel aging and bottle aging. Barrel aging takes place before the wine is bottled, and generally in American or French oak barrels, to mature the wine and concentrate the flavors. Barrel aging can take anywhere from a few months to several years, but even once a wine makes it to the bottle stage, it continues to change and evolve. While white and rosé wine is generally ready to drink shortly after bottling, red wine — particularly heavier reds such as cabernet sauvignon and zinfandel — continue to improve for years when stored under stable conditions. However, every wine does have a peak in quality, after which it begins to deteriorate. When in doubt about the life of a particular wine, consult your local wine shop or call the winery directly.

Balance: The basic attributes of wine — alcohol, acid, tannins and fruit — are a part of every bottle, but they're not always in perfect balance. Sometimes the alcohol overpowers everything else, which tasters refer to as a "hot" wine, or the fruit flavors are overly strong, which is generally called a "fruit bomb." However, when a wine is balanced, all of these elements are synchronized, with no flavor subverting another.

Body: This refers to how the wine feels in the mouth, which is a combination of the wine's alcohol content and acidity, among others. If a wine is considered full-bodied, it usually has a heavy or rich mouthfeel that lingers, while medium- and lighter-bodied wines lean more toward watery, less-complex flavors. In general, red is often considered heavier than white, but chardonnay can be much heavier than a beaujolais nouveau — which is why the old "red with meat, white with fish" rule is too oversimplified for wine pairing.

Bouquet: Also known as aroma or nose, this is the way a wine smells, which is the most important part of tasting. The best way to fully taste a wine is to begin with a big sniff before taking a sip.

Botrytis: This mold, whose full name is botrytis cinerea, is responsible for producing some of the world's most highly coveted dessert wines, including France's Sauternes. It develops when ripe grapes are left on the vine, and it causes the grapes to shrivel, which concentrates the sugars and flavors. It is also referred to as "noble rot."

Breathing: Once a wine is uncorked, oxygen begins entering the wine and changing its flavor. While most white and rosé don't require much air exposure to taste good, fuller-bodied older reds such as cabernet sauvignon can benefit from being open for an hour or so. However, wines that have been in the bottle for several decades will lose their flavor quickly, so connoisseurs know to consume them immediately upon opening.

Brix: The measure of the grapes' sugar content at harvest — the higher the sugar content, the higher the alcohol content of the resulting wine.

Chaptalization: When grapes are harvested early, their sugar content is too low for the yeast to be able to produce a high enough alcohol content during fermentation, so sugar is added to the crushed grapes. Although the practice is illegal in Italy and California, both France and Germany use it successfully, but with restrictions.

Cork Taint: Although wine novices tend to wonder why a sommelier or waiter places the cork on the table and pours a small amount for someone at the table to taste, there's good reason for this little tradition. Not only does an intact cork show that the wine has been well cared for, but the taster can smell a small amount of wine in the glass to determine if a wine has cork taint. Cork taint, which is caused by a bacteria, gives the wine a musty smell reminiscent of wet cardboard. It will not harm humans — but it's definitely not going to improve a meal.

Decant: Decanting consists of pouring the bottle of wine into a wide-bottomed glass or crystal container, which helps get oxygen into the wine quicker. Decanting with a mesh funnel is helpful for unfiltered or moderately old wines, which generally have sediment at the bottom of the bottle. In addition, some wine enthusiasts say that decanting young wines helps make them more palatable.

Filtering: Most wines are filtered just before bottling to ensure that the wines are as clear as possible. This step removes any remaining yeast cells and sediment, but some winemakers believe it also strips the wine of flavor and texture.

Finish: This refers to the taste that lingers in one's mouth upon swallowing the wine. The length of time that the finish lasts can vary depending on the wine.

Magnum: An oversized wine bottle that contains the equivalent of two regular-sized 750ml bottles. But large-format bottles don't end with the magnum: They can range from Jeroboam (4 bottles) to Methuselah (8 bottles) all the way up to Nebuchadnezzer (20 regular-sized bottles).

New World and Old World wines: Terms used frequently in the wine industry. Old World wines usually come from European regions such as France, Italy, Spain and Germany, and they're often labeled for a region instead of the grape. These wines tend to be more subtle, and their acidity makes them pair well with food. New World wines, which include California, Australia and South America, are bolder and heavier than their Old World counterparts. Critics say that New World wines lack the finesse of the Old World, but inexpensive New World wines seem to be what the growing population of wine drinkers gravitate toward.

Phylloxera: This tiny North America-native aphid has caused destruction in the wine world for more than a century by attacking the roots of grape vines, eventually killing the entire vine. Part of phylloxera's insidious nature is that by the time the vine starts to show signs of disease, it's too late to save the vineyard. Many wineries plant the more delicate rosebush at the end of each row of vines because the rose bush will show the effects of phylloxera long before the grape vines, giving the winery a chance to fight off the little bug. If phylloxera takes hold in a vineyard, all of the vines must be ripped out and replanted with American rootstock grafted with vitis vinifera vines on top.

Residual Sugar: For sweeter wines, the fermentation process is halted before the yeast has complete converted the sugar to alcohol. If a wine has a certain percentage of residual sugar, that usually means a sweeter, low-alcohol wine.

Rootstock: This refers to the part of the vine that grows underground. To combat phylloxera, wine grape vines are grafted on to rootstock that would otherwise provide table grapes.

Sediment: Solid matter that remains in wine. Sediment is found in unfiltered wine and older wine, and it's easily removed by pouring the wine through a mesh funnel into a decanter. If you don't decant the wine, be sure to leave the last drops in the bottle to avoid a rather chunky glass of wine.

Sparkling Wine: A generic term that refers to any wine that has bubbles — only wines from the Champagne region of France can be labelled as "Champagne."

Still Wine: Any wine that does not have bubbles.

Tannin: A chemical compound found in the skins, seeds and stems of grapes and in barrels that is extremely beneficial for the structure and aging of red wine. Most white wines have very little tannin.

Terroir: A term originating in France that means a wine will reflect the place in which the grapes are grown.

Varietal: Wine made from a particular kind of grape, be it chardonnay, zinfandel or grenache. Most grapes have a discernible difference from one another, which means that if you don't like a certain cabernet sauvignon, you probably won't like the next one, either.

Vintage: If a year appears on the label of a wine, that indicates the year that the grapes were harvested. A label that doesn't have a vintage usually means that the wine is a blend of grapes from various years.

Vitis Vinifera: All grapevines belong to the genus vitis, but only the vinifera species seem to make good wine. Vinifera includes all of the major wine grapes, including pinot noir, cabernet sauvignon and chardonnay. Most species are native to North America, including vitis labrusca and vitis riparia, both of which provide phylloxera-resistant rootstock to the world.

Sources

We would like to thank the following vineyards for their contributions of courtesy artwork and information:

California:
Ferrari-Carano

Washington:
Chateau Ste. Michelle

Virginia:
Barboursville Vineyards

Idaho:
Sawtooth Winery

France:
Chateau Palmer

Germany:
Mosel
Bruendlymayer

The editors acknowledge, with thanks, all photographs, courtesy:

Dr. Loosen/Dr. Loosen

Kirk Wille/Mozel

Robin Head/ Loosen House

Bruendlymayer

Ferrari-Carano

Chaeteau des Charmes Wines

Barboursville Vineyards

Kevin Cruff/Ste. Michelle

Dale DeGabriele/Sawtooth Winery

Alain Vacheron/Chateau Palmer

Jean Pierre Lagiewski/Chateau Palmer

ASP Editions/Chateau Palmer

Phillippe Roy/Chateau Palmer

Daniel Aron/Chateau Palmer

Special thanks to contributing photographers:

Fernando Bowen, Argentina

Lautaro Colovini, Argentina

Hernan Herrero, Argentina

Konstantinos Dafalias, Austria

Con Mani, Austria

Max Cossio, Chile

Claude Coquilleau, France

Greg MIgeon, France

Christoph Schmitz, Germany

Yiannis Papadimitriou, Greece

Manthy Maragoudaki, Greece

Enzo Cositore, Ireland